UNCOMMON SENSE

Also by James MacGregor Burns

Roosevelt: The Soldier of Freedom

Presidential Government: The Crucible of Leadership

The Deadlock of Democracy: Four-Party Politics in America

John Kennedy: A Political Profile

Roosevelt: The Lion and the Fox

Government by the People (*with Jack W. Peltason*)

Congress on Trial

UNCOMMON SENSE

James MacGregor Burns

HARPER & ROW, PUBLISHERS

New York, Evanston, San Francisco, London

1817

FIRST EDITION

STANDARD BOOK NUMBER: 06–010584–4

LIBRARY OF CONGRESS CATALOG CARD NUMBER: 78–161636

To Gunnar Myrdal

Contents

Foreword   *ix*

PART I

THE LIMITS OF COMMON SENSE

1. THE FAILURE OF THE AMERICAN SYSTEM   4
2. THE ILLUSION OF PRACTICAL PROGRESS   16
3. FOREIGN POLICY: PIETY AND PRACTICE   34
4. OVERTURNING THE SYSTEM   56

PART II

THE PRACTICALITY OF PRINCIPLE

5. THE MOBILIZATION OF CHANGE   77
6. BELIEFS AS GUIDES TO ACTION   92

PART III

THE TASKS OF UNCOMMON SENSE

7. THE TRANSFORMATION OF GOVERNMENT   *113*

8. A PARTY FIT TO GOVERN   *139*

9. THE CRISIS OF LEADERSHIP   *162*

Author's Note   *183*

Reference and Subject Index   *185*

Foreword

I began writing this book during the Mylai trial and am completing it during the aftermath of Attica. The events come as two grim footnotes to a decade of anguish. The tumult and violence that swept through our ghettos, election campaigns, schools, courtrooms, overseas armies, city streets and even our churches has now ended up in our prison yards.

To these symptoms of long, underlying crisis our political leaders have been responding with their usual habits of blandishment, evasion, defensiveness, and delay. A President of the United States, bending to the uproar following the verdict of guilt against Lieutenant Calley by promising to intervene to decide the case personally, robs the event of its only salutary aspect—a nation's decision to try its own soldiers and to parade its own crimes in a public court and before an international tribune of opinion. A world-famous governor of New York, acting on the basis of inadequate if not inaccurate information and inadequate humanity, fails to respond to pleas to come to the field of battle and precipitates a clash that produces the inevitable massacre—defending his course as the only possible alternative.

Even worse, our leaders react to these tragedies not with a determination to confront the underlying causes but with promises to appoint more committees to investigate conditions of which we are only too aware.

For a quarter century I have been criticizing the political system that causes or permits such calamities as Watts, Kent State, Jackson, and Attica, and I withdraw no words I have said; I wish only that I had expressed them more urgently and compellingly. But two developments have convinced me that the liberal reforms we advanced, however desirable in themselves, are inadequate to overcome the persisting deadlock and repeated debacles of the system. One is the obvious fact that the system as a whole is in disarray and we are making little attempt to improve it. The other is a series of personal experiences of the debilitation of key institutions in the system.

Many of us learned of this debilitation also through the misadventures of our children, our students, and their friends—through the young people who were suddenly thrown into confrontation with a law-enforcement system, an educational establishment, a military service, or some other private or public bureaucracy that showed itself utterly incapable of modernizing and rejuvenating itself in the face of new, complex, and sophisticated challenges. The young have been our educators, even when we reject their solutions. Some of us have learned through our own experiences with fumbling, deteriorating institutions—in my case, for example, through intimate exposure to several sectors of not the criminal but the *civil* law and its agencies.

I have come to believe that our *root* troubles lie less in the visible system itself than in the habits of thought that sustain it. As a nation we are experiencing a failure of nerve. We are withdrawing from our national responsibilities at home and abroad because we would rather cling to new and old shibboleths than venture onto uncertain and even dangerous intellectual ground.

This book is a call to undertake that most demanding and revolutionary of all activities—rethinking our goals and our means of attaining them. It proposes that we neither patch up our system nor overthrow it, but that we *transform* it by keeping what is essential to our supreme ends and abandoning anything else that stands in the way. It appeals for the reanimation of our *nationhood*, with all its possibilities for wisdom and for compassion, in a decade that is intended for mere celebration. It dares to say, two hundred years after Tom Paine, that the cause of America is still "in a great measure the cause of all mankind."

J. M. B.

September 1971

Part I

✿

THE LIMITS OF COMMON SENSE

CHAPTER 1

The Failure of the American System

By the start of the 1970s—the decade in which the nation would celebrate its bicentennial—most Americans had lost faith in their political system. The old optimism about the nation's assured and steady progress had eroded, a Gallup poll found; most people felt that their country had lost rather than gained ground in the previous five years, and people expected the United States in 1976, the bicentennial year, to be merely where it had been a decade earlier. About half of the American people feared that social unrest and division was so widespread that a "real breakdown" was likely.

Young people, in particular, were rejecting the system. At the start of the 1970s almost half of more than a thousand students polled on sixty-one campuses thought that change in America over the next quarter century was likely to occur through revolution rather than through relatively peaceful means. Almost half felt that violence was sometimes justified to bring about change in American society. Almost eighty percent said that the American system does not respond quickly enough to the needs of the people.

The reaction to this colossal vote of nonconfidence was curious. Few disputed the essential accuracy of the polls or the significance of the findings. Few even really defended the system. Some commented that the main reason why people felt the system had failed was simple: it *had* failed. But the general reaction was to make a scapegoat of the 1960s. How else could people feel, it was asked, after such a calamitous decade? Almost lovingly, commentators pored through the artifacts of the 1960s—urban decline, rural misery, burning cities, murdered blacks and students, atrocities in southeast Asia, the hooting down of speeches, the disruption of classes, the whole awful array ranging from the evil and sickening to the simply foolish. Many felt that Max Lerner* best summed up the decade: it was the decade of too much power and too much powerlessness, too much affluence and too much hunger, too rich suburbs and too poor inner cities, too much overkill, too big military elites, too big a multiversity, too impersonal a megamachine, too much corruption and hypocrisy, too brief miniskirts and too long maxicoats, too astronomical speeds, too little sense of human limits—and at the end, one might add, too much disillusionment, despair, and bitterness.

Nothing could be expected of a decade, someone said, during which the brains and heart were shot out of three of the most gifted leaders this society could produce—and children were bombed to death in Sunday school.

But did the real crisis come in the 1960s? Or were the 1960s simply a time when all the unresolved past crises boiled up to the surface? Was it indeed, essentially, a period of healthy blowing off of steam that had risen from long-building pressures in society? Perhaps the real crisis was in the 1950s, when government was trying to adjust or repress the forces of social change; or in the 1940s, when enormous social and economic transformations of society advanced beyond governmental foresight and planning; or in the 1920s, when leaders were hardly aware that one of the great migrations of history—rural people into cities, and southern Negroes into northern ghettos—was storing up explosive social forces; or much earlier, in the 1860s, when a northern

* Authors referred to in the text are fully cited in the Reference and Subject Index, as explained in a headnote to the index.

regime was facing the crisis of the Union but evading the even more fundamental crisis of liberty and equality, or in the 1870s, when the victory was dissipated in compromise and repression.

THE SYSTEM IN DECLINE

These questions have a special poignancy as we approach 1976. For that year would commemorate not only the brave deeds of revolutionaries but the daring thought of the 1770s and the decade that followed. The men of 1776 cut through the political shibboleths of their time. The more simple any thing is, said Tom Paine in *Common Sense,* "the less liable it is to be disordered, and the easier repaired when disordered. . . . I offer nothing more than simple facts, plain arguments, and common sense." Although some called for compromise with His Majesty's government, for some kind of arrangement, the self-evident truths of 1776 could be satisfied only by independence.

But the astringent force of common sense was not enough; a vast measure of uncommon sense was necessary to organize a new polity. In writing the Constitution, the Framers acted out of practical experience, but they drew even more deeply from their theories of causation in history, their belief in the possibilities of republican government, their view of the limitations of democracy, their convictions about the nature of man. They were strategists of both revolution and constitution-making. They understood that lofty ends must be related to a realistic measure of human and intellectual resources. Thus they were grand theorists of ends and means, and the Constitution became perhaps the prime example in history of a conscious, considered, deeply theoretical, yet in the long run eminently practical effort to think through national problems and refashion political means to deal with them. For almost two centuries the American experiment has been conducted within the boundaries that the Framers established.

But today our system is being challenged just as sharply as was the colonial system of the 1770s. Voices as blunt and iconoclastic as Tom Paine's characterized—or caricatured—the results of the Grand Experiment on the new continent. Said Julius Lester: "Looking around at this garbage dump called America, blacks thank the Lord each and every day that He didn't make them white." Said a young Mohawk Indian, after dumping sand on Plymouth Rock: "That damned rock! I'd like to blow it up. It was the start of everything bad that has happened to the American Indians." Said Jerry Rubin: "Amerika doesn't have the sniffles or a sore throat, she has malignant cancer."

The defenders of the system, for their part, were confused and demoralized. They were reacting to the symptoms of the 1960s, when the moral bonds holding a people together had seemed to snap. One thinks of that decade and of those who tried to change it—those who entered into public affairs, joined reform groups, sent checks to good causes, took part in political campaigns, kept informed, paid taxes. . . . They had started off that decade by responding to a new young president who asked for service and sacrifice. They lost that leader but then under a new president won a famous victory over embattled conservatism. There followed two years of euphoria as the big bills at last went through Congress. People were not unduly troubled by the upheaval of the blacks. Progress always brought tumult.

But late in the decade everything seemed to come unhinged. The liberal system just did not appear to work. At home, the great social reforms seemed to have little impact; abroad, we were fighting a wretched war we could neither win nor lose. In 1968 a man who for a quarter century had embodied American liberalism, with all its strengths and weaknesses, was beaten at the polls by a man who seemed to represent nothing except imagemaking and remaking. And always we faced the mocking reminder of 1976. Stewart Udall called for Project 76 to make all cities "cathedrals for everyday existence, and to make human relations amicable." But three years after this summons the core cities were in profound crisis. "We surrender," the mayors were saying to Washington. "Treat us like an occupied country after World War II. Give us a Marshall Plan."

WHY THE SYSTEM FAILS

We have failed because we have tried to deal with deeply entrenched, interlocked sets of national problems through sporadic, piecemeal action. We have acted in this fashion because our political institutions are disorganized and fragmented, our leaders improvising and opportunistic, our thinking pragmatic and "practical."

Rarely has a people been so conscious of change as Americans; we constantly talk about it; we flatter ourselves that we understand its imperatives, and we are indeed one of the most innovative nations in the world. But change is something we react to, adjust to; change is personified, reified, even deified. We do not see that change is an infinitely complex set of social processes, that change takes many forms, has many dimensions, moves in mysterious directions, with vagrant and unpredictable results. The issue is not the recognition and ready acceptance of change but whether we can control its processes and channel its forces toward ends we can define and defend. The issue is *directed* change—change harnessed to broadly held ends.

Potentially, the most powerful instrument we have to control change in this fashion is the government. It is the failure of government over the past century to anticipate and manage the enormous social change of that century that most directly lies at the source of our difficulties. The concentration of power in private economic organizations and social structures and in governmental bureaucracies contrasts with the recent drift and instability of executive leadership. While scientific and technical innovation has profoundly altered the distribution of power and the nature of decisionmaking in the new industrial state, government has changed only incrementally. Congress remains an essentially eighteenth-century institution well suited to the family and neighborhood politics of the Whig era in Britain. The presidency has been immensely strengthened as a management institution, but to what ends the vehicle has been better equipped remains obscure. State and local government remains too divided, obsolescent, and impotent to shoulder the burdens assigned by the new federalism.

At the base of the government is a power system as antiquated and ill organized as the government itself. As peoples' needs and as their economic and social arrangements have changed over the past century, one might have expected their institutions at least to adapt to new social forces if not to modify them. But the organization and power of the American party system has hardly changed in over a century, except to become more splintered, less collective, more personalized. Though reform is in the wind for both parties, they are both weak at their foundations—the popular base of the Democrats large but fractured, that of the Republicans shrunken and demoralized. Neither in the nations nor in the states and cities can political leadership find backing for sustained and comprehensive action. Group interests compete, bargain, and coalesce as of old, but they cannot mobilize power to support steady, purposeful action by government. Nor have our political institutions alone failed us. Business has failed to cope with the problem of investment of resources in saving American cities; education has failed to provide for new generations of minority groups the upwardly mobile impetus it gave to earlier generations; religious institutions have faltered in the task of clarifying values and judging public policy; lawyers and doctors have failed to modernize their procedures for dealing with collective needs.

Underlying these political and institutional failures, however, and stunting our capacity to criticize and reform the political system, are crucial failures of thought. Americans have long prided themselves on their common sense, their practicality, their freedom from dogma and even from doctrine. They have glorified the tinkerers, the experimenters, the people who get results, the men of common sense. Long before the writings of Peirce and

James and Dewey and the founding of the new philosophical school of pragmatism, men like Benjamin Franklin and Tom Paine and a thousand less known were demonstrating that the American scene was especially congenial to economic experimentation, technical and social invention, and political improvisation. The almost endless opportunity in the expanding cities and on the frontier, the trading and brokerage of the rising business civilization, the relatively fluid social arrangements, the absence of a single powerful ideology—all these seemed hospitable to open systems of thought and to atomistic change.

These habits of thought dominate the way in which we perceive leaders and problems today. We applaud the practical man, the innovator, the realist. We condemn the idealist, the doctrinaire, the do-gooder. We prefer the tough-minded, the hard-headed, the sharp-witted to the soft-hearted or the tender-minded. We are relieved when some theorist is shown to have a practical side, such as carpentry or gardening, when some moralist comes down to earth, like the preacher who thrashes the bad boys behind the church. Our maxims betray these ways of thinking. Thus some idea—integration, for example—is good in theory but won't work in practice. The proof of the pudding is in the eating (not in the digestion or in the health of the diner). There is no point in standing on principle if it means losing an election. Any religion is good if it works for the person practicing it.

An idea must "work." This means it must produce early, tangible, rewarding, specific results. But for whom? On what field of action? Over what period of time? Above all, measured by what standard or principle? All this is left open. And as we move from the question of what is immediately and literally good for a specific person or group to what is good for a whole people—or for the entire human race—the concept of what works is drained of the very practicality it presumes to exemplify. The history of this nation is studded with actions that seemed wholly practical and beneficial at the time but, in the long run, left a residue of principles violated, hopes defeated, and tasks undone.

The central problem, however, in American thought is not the supremacy of means over ends. It is the disjunction of means and ends. It is the conduct of one line of activity on the basis of what specifically and narrowly works, and another line of affirmation and rhetoric that may be designed simply to meet the people's need for official piety. Most of the philosophical pragmatists recognized this. "For Dewey, wherever action is intelligent and responsible, the means are a part of the ends," Sidney Hook has said. "We do not know what we have chosen unless we see what is involved in bringing that choice about; we cannot proclaim allegiance to exalted ideals as if that freed us from the moral imperative of judging them by their consequences." And once one speaks of consequences, rather than immediate practical results, he is talking of things that matter to most of us, and over the long run.

But what to do? The very complexity of the 1960s has made analysis difficult. "There is something awesome and baffling about a society," Zbigniew Brzezinski said, "that can simultaneously change men's relationship to the universe by placing a man on the moon, wage and finance a thirty-billion-dollar-per-annum foreign war despised by significant portions of its people, maintain the most powerful and far-flung military forces in history, and confront in the streets and abet in the courts a revolution in its internal racial relations, doing all this in the context of the explosion of higher learning in its rapidly expanding and turbulent universities, of rotting urban centers, of fumbling political institutions, and of dynamically growing frontier industries that are transforming the way its citizens live and communicate with one another."

THE TWO CLOCKS

Analysis of our ailments and prescriptions for cure have been as varied and complex as the society examined. Some are psychological or sociological. Our troubles stem from too much permissiveness, or from lack of a masculine presence in the family, or from various forms of anomie or alienation, or the loss of community, or the decline of the American spirit, or from corruption by television and the other mass media, or from the subjugation of women, or sexual inadequacy. There are economic theories: uncontrolled technology, the contradictions of capitalism, rule by the industrial-military complex, too much spending (or too little), the perversion of economic and political priorities; the population explosion; the migration to the cities, the migration of whites out of the core city. "More and more of us," Andrew Hacker complained, "are now part-time sociologists; we have no difficulty in dilating on all manner of crises ranging from poverty and civil liberties to pollution and violent crime." We remember a warning by C. Wright Mills: "If there is any one line of orientation historically implicit in American social science, surely it is the bias toward scattered studies, toward factual surveys and the accompanying dogma of a pluralist confusion of causes. These are essential features of liberal practicality as a style of social study."

What, then, are we to do in the face of so many and such varied analyses? It is not as though the investigators fail in their inquiries or prescriptions. On the contrary, most of the lines of reform I have listed so summarily represent impressive theoretical and empirical work by some of the nation's—and the world's—ablest social theorists. Most of them believe that, like true radicals, they are digging into the root of things, and many indeed are. But what are we to think? What are we to do? In this endless debate among scholars as to the true cause of our malaise, can we wait for a verdict? Will there be time for a verdict? Or will we be in a position, as Auden warned, of lecturing on navigation while the ship is going down?

To make matters worse, we sense that there is no single "cause" of our troubles but rather a tangle of causes. When we seem to have located main causes and ancillary causes we suspect that all are so interrelated, so mutually reinforcing and balancing and thwarting, that we can never measure exactly what specifically caused what. Social scientists who explore even the simplest of causal phenomena find that the factors are numerous and clouded; they offer not hard explanations but probabilities and tendencies.

Hence we do not wait—quite sensibly—for the final explanations to come in. As "practical" people we roll up our sleeves, put our shoulder to the wheel, and improve matters where we can. We patch things up here and there, paste over a few problems we can't seem to solve, touch up, redecorate, camouflage. But now we discover that practicality is not enough. Things do not fundamentally improve. Poverty continues. Crime and violence flourish. The environment deteriorates further. Poor blacks go on migrating into the city and affluent whites into the suburbs.

We seem to be caught between two worlds, one dying and the other waiting to be born, but beyond that we have discovered that even our time scales have failed us. "The time outlooks of the scholar-scientist and of the practical men of affairs who surround the world of science tend to be different," Robert Lynd said. "The former works in a long, leisurely world in which the hands of the clock crawl slowly over a vast dial; to him, the precise penetration of the unknown seems too grand an enterprise to be hurried, and one simply works ahead within study walls relatively sound-proofed against the clamorous urgencies of the world outside. . . . The practical man of affairs, on the other hand, works by a small time-dial over which the second-hand of immediacy hurries incessantly, 'Never mind the long past and the infinite future,' insists the clattering little monitor, 'but do this, fix this—now, before tomorrow morning.' "

"PROBE YOUR MAIN ROOTS"

How do we get out of a trap that seems both intellectual and institutional? Our very words of discourse are suspect. Nothing epitomized the recent decade better than the Tower of Babel. We saw the high-blown, synthetic rhetoric of the politicians seldom translated into equivalent deeds. We were lost among what

C. Wright Mills called sponge words—pompous words like *partnership, consensus, imperialism, relevance*—words now drained of meaning. The chaos of sound has intensified the chaos of our thought. We needed rational language that sought to communicate ideas, not pulverize the opposition.

But clarity of language is not itself enough. Clarity of purpose is called for. Radical rethinking is required because history advances by geometric progression. The clock is speeding up. We must go beyond the usual national stocktaking, which inquires whether the nation is using appropriate means for given ends. We must reexamine the ends themselves, beginning with the values that lie deep in the American heritage. "Probe the earth and see where your main roots are," Thoreau urged. I will contend that if we do, we will rediscover collective values that give clear guidelines to the American purpose today—guides that in turn can help set national priorities. From those ends the means will follow, and hence our task is to reformulate the entire structure of goals and the methods to attain them.

New priorities will be derived from that new synthesis:

First, the absolute, uncompromising defense of *individual liberty,* from negative liberties, such as the right of privacy, to positive liberties, like the right to demonstrate against the government. Second, *equality*—the expansion of social, economic, and political rights to provide for all Americans genuine equality of opportunity and a far greater equality of condition, in the sense that no American will lack resources necessary for a decent life and none should be so poor that the differences in income are a national infamy. This means, of course, the categorical abolition of poverty in the United States.

These two great priorities are a necessary and logical derivation of liberty and equality. But the strategies that will be discussed here as necessary to overcome poverty can be used to solve other priority problems rising from deeply entangled social and political ills: crime and violence, economic recession, wretched education, environmental blight, drug addiction, business and industrial concentration, the military (or the military-industrial, or the military-industrial-congressional) complex, the aesthetic drabness that afflicts so much of America. All these are consequences of the derangement of fundamental values and the substitution of lesser priorities. Everyone is entitled to his own set of priorities. I rate the environment as the highest priority, behind liberty and equality, but all three of these are related. (1) To protect and enhance the environment is to enhance individual liberty in its most creative aspects and to insist on economic equality; the poor, for example, suffer the most from environmental deterioration; (2) to deal with the environment as comprehensively as we must is to deal necessarily with problems of poverty, education, aesthetics; (3) to emphasize the environment—ecology, conservation, recreation, wildlife, open country, orderly expansion and development—is to conserve and nurture the world of human beings. All this has culminated in our time in a concern that may become for the late twentieth century the compelling vision that the great Enlightenment values were for the eighteenth.

Others may have a different order of priorities, but the point is that there must *be* an order of priorities that can be actually realized through whatever changes in means that the reformulated ends require. It is the effort to think and to govern without a considered order of principles and achievable priorities that has so often reduced our politics to triviality and our government to impotence on the great human issues.

The time has come to strive for *un*common sense. We must work out *strategies* of directed change and progress—strategies that combine ends and means, thought and action, theory and practicality. We have hardly begun to think through these strategic possibilities. We have felt limited to two unhappy alternatives: one, the slow but steady accretion of progress achieved by limited manipulation of the existing structures of government and society; the other, the desperate precipitation of change and reform by rejecting the existing structures and acting outside them. But each of these alternatives presents a disjunction of ends and means. We must search for a third strategy that will truly put first things first—that will define its ends and shape the means to realize them.

"A people that can face itself in the dark mirror of a time like ours is a great people which deserves to be greatly represented," Archibald MacLeish says. "It is capable of mastering its destiny. But to master destiny is to *act*, and the American bicentennial should be framed in action, not a backward-looking self-congratulation on a past we have ourselves betrayed, but a new beginning, a second struggle to achieve that noblest and most difficult of all human dreams."

CHAPTER 2

The Illusion of Practical Progress

Ideas have consequences. Perhaps the most dangerous application of a simplistic, pragmatic, commonsense approach to our public affairs has been its impact on domestic policy. Here American government and business have disrupted the proper interrelation of means and ends by elevating means to the status of ends. Thus the process of profitmaking became a goal in itself. Even seemingly benign devices—redistribution of resources as in many income maintenance plans, for example—did not provide a rigorous consideration of the ends implicit in such devices and of alternative ends that might, if recognized, demand different means. Liberals with their bread-and-butter issues, conservatives with their protectionist or laissez-faire policies that benefited the minority—both made the mistake of expecting too much of process in itself. And then in the 1960s they compounded the error by subordinating quantitative economic issues to so-called qualitative ones without ever having come to grips with the quantitative.

Years before, John Maynard Keynes had observed that the "day is not far off when the Economic Problem will take the back seat where it belongs, and that the arena of the heart and head will be occupied, or reoccupied, by our real problems—the problems of life and human relations, of creation and behavior and religion." Keynes had helped make that new day possible. By the 1960s liberals were making a major distinction between the "old" economic issues of gross national product, poverty, affluence, wages, social security, taxation—the *size* and *apportioning* of the cake of affluence—and the "new" issues of privacy, sexual tolerance, ecology, government support of the arts, nonconformity in behavior, books, films, and others—the *style* and *taste* of the cake. And conservatives were alarmed by the near-collapse of law and order, by student rebellion, ghetto turmoil, the spread of pornography, and the decline of public courtesy and private morality, while subordinating the issues of recession, black unemployment, poverty, tax inequities, and the like. Neither side had a firm grip on the relation between its goals and its means.

ECONOMIC OR MORAL PROGRESS?

Those of us who predicted the ascendancy of the new issues of quality and "style of life" and gave them our closest attention made two mistakes. In the euphoria of the 1960s economic boom that had touched millions of Americans, we assumed that the basic quantitative problems had been solved or were in the process of being overcome. In fact we ended up in 1968 with only slightly decreased poverty, with an inflation that afflicted the urban poor in particular, and with a series of other dire economic problems. The War on Poverty had ended not with victory but with an armistice. By the end of the decade President Nixon had, in addition, achieved a recession. Presiding over both a slump *and* an inflation was a feat of quantitative pyrotechnics, but not one that any would boast about. By decade's end labor and capital and other groups were resuming their fight over the size and shares of the cake with as much zest as ever. Nixon's price and wage freeze would only postpone the struggle.

This error of prediction had a grievous dimension. Many assumed that if the economy had brought us new affluence and its accompanying satisfactions, it had done so for virtually all the people. But here we were a victim of class and racial blindness. While we grew affluent, the rural and ghetto poor were hardly touched. The rate of unemployment of young black males in the urban ghettos ranged far above the level of nationwide unemployment. While young white liberals on college campuses shifted from civil rights to ecology and women's liberation and sexual freedom, ghetto riots were a shocking reminder that the quality-of-life issues were a luxury for those who saw economic survival itself as a fragile hope.

The second mistake was a mirror image of the first. Somehow we had assumed that when qualitative issues came to predominate they would be *our* qualitative issues—tame, benign, civilized issues like civil liberties and the environment. And we assumed that the great mass of people would be on our side on these issues. In fact the dominant qualitative, style-of-life issues of the late 1960s turned out to be the *conservatives'* issues—crime, violence, permissiveness, pornography, drugs, sexual freedom. These issues were at the heart of Nixon's strategy in 1968.

Thus, by the end of the 1960s, the nation had come to grips with neither the old agenda of economic problems nor the new agenda of style of life or morality. What had seemed an orderly way to deal with these agendas—sequentially, with economics first and then, after the cake was bigger and the shares fairer, to advance to qualitative matters—had proved to be impossible. The nation had to deal with both agendas at the same time. But it had not faced the reason for the failures of the strategy and hence was doomed to repeat them, in new guises, unless the old and new issues were candidly engaged. Even more, the illusion of practical progress that had made it possible for us to "graduate" from quantitative issues before they were resolved for Americans as a whole suggested that the people and their leaders were capable of distorting qualitative issues as well. The failure to understand and acknowledge the importance of ends had served reactionary interests primarily, as it usually will, for unacknowledged ends camouflage the probably conservative consequences of means.

Still, we must not saddle this generation, suffering from an overload of guilt as it is, with more than its share of blame. The illusion of practical progress is not a new phenomenon. Looking back two centuries, we see that the Founding Fathers, despite all their vision and brilliance, on at least one matter preferred common to uncommon sense. And, subsequently, the most successful presidents and other political leaders failed to unite effectively their ends and means, while the less successful, including Mr. Nixon, seemed to lack any coherent ends by which their means could be shaped. Pragmatism, too, is as American as apple pie.

THE MUTED CRY

Liberalism, said Ortega y Gasset, "is the supreme form of generosity; it is the right which the majority concedes to minorities and hence it is the noblest cry that has ever resounded in this planet. It announces the determination to share existence with the enemy; more than that, with an enemy which is weak. . . ." From the outset Americans faced a dilemma that would harshly test their capacity to shape means to fit their libertarian and egalitarian ends. The dilemma lay first in the institution of slavery and, later, in the practices of segregation and discrimination. The Negro has posed the supreme moral issue for American democracy because he is black, he is poor, he is generally powerless, and because he has been denied both the liberty and the equality that lie at the heart of the American credo.

The men of 1776 and 1787 were children of the Enlightenment. In drawing up the Declaration and the Constitution they spoke out of deep convictions about liberty and equality. But they faced a practical problem—the Declaration had to be approved by the Continental Congress and the Constitution ratified by the states. In drafting the Declaration Jefferson wrote a full paragraph attacking the king for waging "cruel war against human nature itself, violating its most sacred rights of life and liberty in the persons of distant people, who never offended him, captivating and carrying them into slavery in another hemisphere, or to incur miserable death in their transportation thither. . . ." This assault on the slave trade was struck out in Philadelphia in deference to certain "Southern gentlemen" and to some northerners uneasy about Yankee complicity in the slave trade. The Constitution presented the same moral dilemma but in different guise: how much congressional representation for southern slaves? Delegates from southern states with large numbers of slaves wanted them to be counted in order to swell southern representation in the House of Representatives; the Framers agreed that a slave should count as three-fifths of a person—but, of course, the slave would not vote.

This Solomon-like compromise set the style for a series of practical settlements over the next seventy years—territorial, sectional, and legal settlements that political brokers hoped would mark the end of the problem. It took a man of Jefferson's prescience to see, as he did in 1821, "the speck on our horizon which is to burst on us as a tornado, sooner or later." In the end, all the commonsense arrangements proved to have a Cervantean "practicality of madness" as the tornado struck soon after Lincoln took office.

Lincoln understood the moral dimensions of the Civil War. "This is essentially a people's contest," he told Congress. "On the side of the Union it is a struggle for maintaining in the world that form and substance of a government whose leading object is to elevate the condition of men. . . ." If this was Lincoln's ultimate end, how well did he make his operationalism serve this end? The end itself was somewhat blurred because Lincoln, with his border-state background and reservations about racial integration, had been mainly concerned about the future of free white labor, not the blacks, and he favored colonization abroad. But as the Civil War became more and more a struggle not just to preserve the Union but to elevate the Negro out of servitude, Lincoln became more involved in the popular commitment to emancipation and to equality for blacks.

However, Lincoln faced a host of practical problems—problems of managing the war, keeping or winning support in the border states, placating northern moderates, conducting diplomacy with other nations. To manage such problems it was necessary to put the instrumental end of union over the ultimate ends of liberty and equality. In answer to a plea by Horace Greeley—"The Prayer of Twenty Millions"—Lincoln wrote: "My paramount object in this struggle *is* to save the Union, and is *not* either to save or destroy slavery. If I could save the Union without freeing *any* slave I would do it, and if I could save it by freeing *all* the slaves I would do it; and if I could save it by freeing some and leaving others alone I would also do that. What I do about slavery, and the colored race, I do because I believe it helps to save the Union; and what I forbear, I forbear because I do *not* believe it would help to save the Union. . . ." The president never wavered in his subordination of the race issue.

The supreme defense of Lincoln's operationalism lay in the proposition that if he could save the Union he could save the prime instrument—a strong national government ruling a reunited North and South—indispensable for achieving all the ultimate ends of the American venture. A broken nation, on the other hand, could achieve no goals. The first test of this proposition came in the treatment of the freedmen after the Civil War. At last the North had the constitutional power and much of the economic and social resources necessary to achieve the now paramount end of liberty and equality for the Negro. But the story of Reconstruction illustrates again the indivisibility of ends and means—in this case, how Lincoln's operationalism carried over into the postwar policy toward the freedmen and fatally affected it. He had been so concerned during the war to take moderate means—for example, in favor of states' rights, including southern states' rights—that the North ended the war without clear guidance from the fallen leader whose prestige had been immensely heightened as to postwar policies that might carry out the great moral commitment of the North to the emancipated blacks. On balance, Lincoln's wartime policy hindered the enactment of the humane and creative policies that might have been possible, given the state of northern feeling and northern resources. Many postwar leaders, especially among the radicals, wanted to reorganize southern society; to distribute land to the freedmen; to outlaw discrimination at the polls, in education, in public places. They saw not only the peril of leaving the former slaveowning class in power in the South but the fearful consequences of perpetuating in Congress the southern delegations representing the old oligarchies and now actually enjoying increased numbers in Congress as a result of the abolition of the provisions for three-fifths representation for slaves. When national authority was finally brought to bear on the Confederacy, hopes for a bold and sweeping political reorganization of the South perished in struggles over less crucial matters, such as punishing the old elite or the alleged misdeeds of black and white politicians. It is not surprising that, toward the end, Lincoln said: "I claim not to have controlled events but confess plainly that events have controlled me."

BETWEEN MASTERY AND SPASM

The twentieth century has produced a number of vigorous presidents who proposed to control events through the forthright executive deployment of enhanced national power. It also produced less activist presidents who were wary of untrammeled presidential authority. The tragedy of the century is not that presidents of the latter type failed to attack the roots of black deprivation—they made no pretense of trying to do so—but that the *activist* presidents in both parties who took moral stands and made political commitments on the issue also failed.

Theodore Roosevelt represented the party that had created a coalition of Negroes, northern labor, businessmen, western farmers, and Civil War veterans; he, like Lincoln, was eager for the elevation of men; he gave Negro Republicans patronage jobs in the South; and, to the consternation of the racists, he invited Booker T. Washington to lunch at the White House. He seems to have had little personal racial prejudice; he wrote Owen Wister that "I do not know a white man of the South who is as good a man as Booker Washington today." But he admired Washington because the black leader was trying to fit the Negro to "do ever better industrial work"; he considered Negroes an inferior race to whites; and at best he took a paternalistic attitude toward blacks and seemed to support racial segregation. It was hard to discern much connection between Roosevelt's moral posturing on the one hand and his specific policies and attitudes on the other. It can be said of his position on black equality, as Morison has commented more generally, that "it has no decent intellectual underpinning; in vain one scrutinizes the scheme to find a logically constructed system of ideas. There is no organized statement of self-evident truths about man and his requirements to provide a direction or a basis for judgment in political action. . . ."

The New Freedom that Woodrow Wilson enunciated in the campaign of 1912 had no clear place for the minority that would most have benefited from it. Despite his own southern background and attitudes, Wilson readily accepted the support of such advocates of racial equality as W. E. B. Du Bois and Oswald Garrison Villard. Soon after Wilson's inauguration, Villard won from him what the NAACP leader considered to be an agreement to accept Villard's plan for the establishment by the president of a national commission to study the whole problem of race relations. A few months later Wilson reneged on the matter; he told Villard that appointment of such a commission would arouse resentment among southern congressmen and jeopardize the administration's legislative program. Wilson also favored segregation of employees in federal agencies—for the benefit of the Negroes, he explained—and allowed segregation in Washington bureaus and actual downgrading and discharge of blacks in southern offices until a howl of outrage from northern progressives brought an end to the policy.

That most practical of decisions—denying or evading Negro demands for liberty and equality on the grounds that southern members of Congress would retaliate against the president's program—became the easy apology of later Democratic administrations. Franklin Roosevelt brought to the White House a baffling compound of personal compassion for Negroes, a degree of social paternalism, sensitivity to their increasing political articulateness, and a personal hatred of racism. Negro leaders were impressed by the concern that many administration officials exhibited for black needs and rights. But administration was one thing, legislation another. By 1935—a year in which blacks were lynched at the rate of about one every three weeks—Negroes were pressing for enactment of an antilynching bill and were running into the usual southern filibuster in the Senate. Eleanor Roosevelt brought NAACP leader Walter White to the White House. "I did not choose the tools with which I must work," the President told White. "But I've got to get legislation passed by Congress to save America." Because of the seniority rule, he said, southerners had control of most of the Senate and House committees. "If I come out for the anti-lynching bill now, they will block every bill I ask Congress to pass to keep America from collapsing. I just can't take that risk."

However justified, this argument could of course be trotted out every year—there was always an important legislative program before Congress. The coming of world war and national emergency gave black leaders a greater opportunity to realize their aims through executive action. In the spring of 1941, angered by discrimination in defense industries and, even, in federally sponsored training and employment programs, White and others urged the president to abolish discrimination in all federal agencies by executive order. Little was forthcoming except promises. As a last resort, A. Philip Randolph of the Sleeping Car Porters proposed a march on Washington unless the administration set up an antidiscrimination program with teeth. The president saw such a move as a blow to the image of national unity he had been shaping. Through Eleanor Roosevelt he sent word that the march might set back progress that had been made in the army, at least against segregation, and might arouse in Congress "even more solid opposition from certain groups than we have had in the past." But Randolph and White stood their ground. The march was called off only when the president promised to issue an executive order against discrimination, which he did in June 1941.

It was a small step forward. The new Committee on Fair Employment Practice had very little enforcement power, funds, or staff; it would be frustrated by labor and business as well as southern conservatism; the president gave it limited support. But the first little step had been taken, and in the 1944 election campaign Roosevelt proposed that FEPC be made permanent. With these precedents established, Harry Truman was able to move ahead in the spirit of the fallen leader. When Congress, only two months after Roosevelt's death, refused to appropriate funds for the FEPC, the new president, by executive order, established a new agency for the same purpose, though still with limited power. Taking the step Wilson had refused to take, Truman set up a Commission on Civil Rights, many of whose recommendations for stronger federal action for civil rights he passed on to Congress, which routinely voted them down or failed to act.

By the 1950s the federal government was beginning to move; the question now was whether it could act boldly and comprehensively and speedily enough to head off the gathering crisis over the denial of Negro rights. President Eisenhower, by evading the crucial moral issue of black inequality and oppression, temporized in the face of this challenge. Although he appointed Earl Warren as chief justice, he scarcely could have foreseen that this California Republican would lead a united Court to the greatest single national affirmation of liberty and equality in a century—an affirmation rivaling the economic and social commitment of the New Deal. Eisenhower's administration maintained the New Deal–Fair Deal momentum on civil rights in some respects, but perhaps most significant was his reluctance to send federal troops into Little Rock to enforce the orders of the Court, and his announcement that he was taking action not necessarily because he believed in it but because he was required to do so under the Constitution. For all his pietism and rhetoric about American values, he did not believe that the president should take strong leadership on matters of specific principle. He did act, but the temporizing—and the rationale behind it—underlined the reluctance of American political leadership over the decades to confront this grievous issue with candor and with power.

It was essentially on this issue of moral leadership and presidential assertiveness that John F. Kennedy based his campaign in 1960. "I am no Whig," he had said a year before his election, and during the campaign he proclaimed that he wanted to be a president "who has the confidence of the people—and who takes the people into his confidence—who lets them know what he is doing and where we are going, who is for his program and who is against. I hope to set before the people our unfinished agenda—to indicate their obligations—and not simply follow their every whim and pleasure. . . . I am not promising action in the first 100 days alone—I am promising you 1,000 days of exacting presidential leadership." He took an advanced position on civil rights, criticizing the Eisenhower administration for avoiding opportunities for ending discrimination in federal housing, which "the President could do by a stroke of his pen," pledging to offer leadership and direction if he was elected, and noting that the "Negro baby has one-half, regardless of his talents, statistically has one-half as much chance of finishing high school as the white baby, one-third as much chance of finishing college, one-fourth as much chance of being a professional man or woman, four times as much chance of being out of work."

But even with this vibrant, activist young president it was the same old story of compromise and delay. He did seize myriad opportunities to advance civil rights in his appointments, in executive orders (except for the "stroke of the pen"), and in symbolic actions, but he held back from the crucial step of presenting a strong legislative program on civil rights to Congress and putting his full political weight behind it. Both black and white experts, both inside and outside the government, were urging him that while no single approach would bring an end to discrimination—since inequalities in black voting, education, employment, housing, and the administration of justice all reinforced one another—Negro political participation was probably the first and crucial step that would make the others far more possible. Still Kennedy held back, even though southern Democrats in Congress were far less hostile to voting legislation than to education and housing. He postponed action for a familiar reason: he needed congressional support on other measures.

Negro leaders applauded Kennedy's personal concern even while they despaired over his failure to make a policy commitment. Martin Luther King, Jr., feared that civil rights was being displaced as the dominant issue of conscience in the nation because token victories were being accepted as indications of genuine progress. The civil rights movement, he said, "instead of breaking out into the open plains of progress, remains constricted and confined. A sweeping revolutionary force is pressed into a narrow tunnel." Sit-ins, demonstrations, marches, killings were spreading through the South.

In mid-1963 the president took the whole issue to the people as "a moral issue . . . as old as the scriptures and . . . as clear as the American Constitution." The time had come for the nation to meet its great commitment. "A great change is at hand, and our task, our obligation, is to make that revolution, that change, peaceful and constructive for all." Soon he sent new civil rights proposals to Congress. But even these proposals were not as strong as later experience proved would be needed, and in any case the time had grown fearfully late. The backlash was already under way. Black leaders were now planning a march on Washington, and Kennedy was almost as worried about this as Roosevelt had been twenty-two years before. He feared its impact on Congress, but the civil rights movement went ahead, the president cooperated, Congress accepted the demonstration in good spirit, and by late November the administration's moderate civil rights measures were on the floor of the House. But by now it was too late for John F. Kennedy.

The slain president had set the stage well for his successor, and Lyndon B. Johnson was eager to attest his own commitment against black inequality and deprivation. He grasped the nettle of racism most of his predecessors had merely touched. As a southerner he had seen and felt the guilt of racial injustice; as the president now of all the people he felt a moral obligation to reform action. In his first term he made civil rights his domestic top priority. "We shall overcome," he proclaimed, and he stirred new hope in the black community just as the War Against Poverty, also bequeathed from the Kennedy administration, did among the nation's poor. His appointment of Thurgood Marshall to the Supreme Court superbly linked practical and symbolic action with moral ends. But too soon, with his reverses in the congressional elections of 1966 and with practical men recommending a return to gradualism, he fell back on his old style of political consensus and compromise. The major civil rights legislation that began to go through Congress stirred new hope that the nation at last was catching up with its moral obligations, but black unrest and resistance was starting to overflow the channels of orderly reform. An attempt by education officials to compel moves toward integration in Chicago backfired in the face of the power of the city organization. The efforts of antipoverty officials to carry out the total war he had declared ran afoul of divisive and competing local forces. Money desperately needed to back up the big new domestic programs began to flow toward the spreading war in Indochina. By 1968 the record of the Johnson administration in civil rights was one of triumph and tragedy.

At least Johnson had acted dauntlessly and with political impact; the coming of the Nixon administration brought a return to the devices of realism, practicality, and compromise. Racial insensitivity in high places contaminated welfare and housing policies; benign neglect helped shape budget priorities. Only the most practical type of miscalculation made possible the nominations of men like Carswell and Haynesworth to the Supreme Court. But perhaps the most dramatic manifestation of the Nixon administration's lack of principled ends was its ambivalent and tortuous policy on school integration, especially the issue of busing. Although millions of American children are bused to public, parochial, and private schools every day and take this as a matter of course, Nixon chose to challenge busing for the achievement of school integration as a social evil of the most malignant sort, damaging to neighborhood and family. By insisting that busing be rejected as an option for integration unless strictly ordered by the courts, and by threatening his own staff with dismissal if they ordered it, he created political turmoil in southern school systems that had been valiantly striving to adjust to integration. He undermined liberal progress in the South as well, and he threatened the very structure of law and order that he had so often apotheosized. In diminishing the values of equality and justice, he stimulated the most disreputable political and social forces to offer themselves as eager allies with conservative Republicans. George Wallace said that he held the federal courts of the nation "in contempt." It was the president of the United States who had made it politically possible across the nation for him to do so.

THE REALISTS

All these presidents were practical men. They would never have reached the White House had they not proved their ability to assess political situations realistically, gather equally hard-headed men around them, bargain and pressure and maneuver, and get results, like winning elections. Most if not all of them were also men of goodwill, of sincerity. They wanted to do good, to carry out their promises, to achieve a record of progress, to go down in history as leaders who had improved the lot of their people, perhaps of all mankind. Most left office feeling that they had, indeed, achieved a good deal of practical progress.

Perhaps they had. But looking back from the vantage point of the 1970s we know that this practical progress was far too slow, too uneven, too short-range, too piecemeal and transient to begin to anticipate, plan against, come to grips with, and resolve the economic and social crises that have been developing in this country for over a century. The failures in civil rights are only the most dramatic of many examples; medical care, public housing, the protection of the civil liberties of the poor and the powerless, environmental control, the simple direction and management of the economy, as President Nixon's floundering has again demonstrated—these are other items on a long list.

Or consider simply one policy—though a crucial one for other programs—our experience with redistribution of income. Twenty years ago Frederick Lewis Allen spoke for the conventional wisdom of the day when he wrote that "we had brought about a virtually automatic redistribution of income from the well-to-do to the less well-to-do." Only in recent years have we become aware that our tax system, instead of being the progressive instrument we assumed, in fact was not an important means for redistributing income from the rich and middle-income to the poor. The main effect had been a small improvement in the income of middle-class groups at the expense of the rich *and* the poor. All sorts of practical things are done—graduated income taxes are passed, social services expanded, welfare programs broadened, wars on poverty declared—and we continue year after year, decade after decade, with a highly inegalitarian income structure.

Why? How can this happen with realists in charge? How can we get such impractical results when men of practicality are doing their level best? Challenged on this score, the realists would have ready answers. Presidents, for example, would point to the fact that the party that was able to help elect them to office had not been very helpful in putting programs through. They would note that a conservative coalition in Congress had been able to delay and destroy administration measures. Most of all they would point to the fact that a president must work along a wide front, seeking public, legislative, bureaucratic, and intellectual support for an immense variety of projects. The priorities that can be imagined so easily by the outsider cannot be marshaled and carried out so effectively at the center of the web of constraints.

Much of this defense is plausible. The question is how much the presidents have been at the mercy of the obstructive forces because of their own inability to put first things first, to work out the relations between their ends and means. During the course of John Kennedy's administration four Kennedys seemed to be emerging—rhetorical radical, policy liberal, fiscal moderate, and institutional conservative. From a perspective of ten years this judgment need not be markedly revised, only extended. For Roosevelt, Truman, Johnson each, in varying degrees, embraced these four roles, though none perhaps so notably as Kennedy. Nixon combined at least three of them, in different degrees and with different results.

With all the avowed liberals, at least, the failure was not essentially one of honesty or concern; it was not *mainly* a failure of the system or of the presidents' failures to challenge it directly. It was mainly a failure of strategy, a failure to establish priorities drawn from an overall purpose that, in turn, stemmed from a set of overriding national goals. The activist presidents, to be sure, tended to move leftward during their administrations, but always they stayed within the constraining parameters of the system. Wilson shifted toward urban progressivism but could not bring his nineteenth century, agrarian-based party with him. Roosevelt abolished the two-thirds rule in the Democratic convention; he challenged the Supreme Court and congressional conservatives in his own party, but neither successfully. He tried, on the whole, to govern within the system and manipulated it with great finesse even while he was ultimately defeated by it. Kennedy felt handicapped by his tenuous popular margin over Nixon and by the anti-New Frontier congressional Democrats entrenched in the power centers on Capitol Hill. He made the decision early in his presidency to conciliate and compromise with Congress, on Jefferson's dictum that great innovations should not be forced on slender majorities. Perhaps he would have made a breakthrough if he had lived to combat and defeat Barry Goldwater in 1964, but unless he altered the system itself, spasms of government action would doubtless have been succeeded once again by the draining negativism of the system. Each of these men had good if cloudy ends; not one of them could command the means to serve his ends.

All this is a weakness of the American presidency, not merely of the local politicians who must necessarily run variously with the hares and the hounds. All this is a weakness of the "most powerful office in the free world," the "mainspring of American government," the "centerpiece of the federal system." The mainspring has not been able to keep all the other parts of the government in steady motion. The overpromising and overselling by rhetorical radicals aspiring to the White House contrasted with the underperformance by economically and institutionally conservative politicians in the office; the incrementalism that has made programs too little and too late in attacking entrenched deprivation; the failure of the national government to plan comprehensively; the endless bargaining between the White House and other power centers, with the resulting policy reflecting the lowest common denominator; the presidential lust for consensus rather than simple popular majorities to legitimate actions; the elephantiasis of government that produces more and more dispersed power centers but not effective administration; the eternal trading and brokerage in the administration that drains programs of their impact and focus—all these have helped produce a crisis of public authority in America, a pervasive popular cynicism as to the capacity of the "system" and a yearning on the part of many Americans to reject the system and to function outside it. Only a reconciliation of means with ends, of private and public institutions with the national purpose at its best, could dispel the illusion of practical progress and replace it with the reality of consistent social advance.

CHAPTER 3

Foreign Policy: Piety and Practice

In some of his last writings on foreign policy before joining President Nixon's staff, Henry Kissinger returned to a question that had long preoccupied him and is the central problem of this book—the relation between ends and means in American statecraft. He coolly dissected the practices and thinking that, he felt, had crippled our foreign policymaking—the haziness of our national objectives; the emphasis on short-run, manageable goals; the absence of well-ordered priorities; the failure to anticipate and plan against crises; the bureaucratic erosion of innovation and leadership; the instinct toward gradualism—all of which had produced, among other things, an alternation of rigidity and spasm in American diplomacy.

The American "bureaucratic-pragmatic leadership," he said, assumed an ad hoc and pragmatic approach toward policy. "Because pragmatism is based on the conviction that the context of events produces a solution, there is a tendency to await developments. The belief is prevalent that every problem will yield if attacked with sufficient energy. It is inconceivable, therefore, that delay might result in irretrievable disaster; at worst it is thought to require a redoubled effort later on. Problems are segmented into constituent elements, each of which is dealt with by experts in the special difficulty it involves. There is little emphasis or concern for their interrelationship. Technical issues enjoy more careful attention, and receive more sophisticated treatment, than political ones. . . ."

Now, some years after these words were written, it does not seem surprising that the early, Harvard Kissinger and the later, White House Kissinger reasoned on different levels of perspective and insight. This is a familiar problem encountered by many who have moved from a secure role as critic and scholar to the uneasy responsibilities of involved observer, of partner in the making of policy and the exercise of power. Americans have assumed a necessary dichotomy between the critic or the idealist, privileged to judge from a protected enclave of no responsibility, and the political leader, whose ignoring or compromising of lofty values endorsed on the campaign trail is excused as "realistic." The exercise of power is widely assumed to be in conflict with adherence to principle. The "responsible" wielder of power, whether a corporation executive, university chancellor, or American president, is regarded as being responsible and even statesmanlike, in contrast to being naïve and softheaded, to the extent that he departs from principle as he feels necessary to appease or balance or postpone conflicting interests. He is expected to obscure values rather than illuminate them, to adapt principle to practice rather than practice to principle.

In the realm of foreign policy, this failure to act on principle is camouflaged by dogmatic sloganeering (e.g., the fight of the Free World against Communism), which on the one hand limits the practical options of strategy that would enhance real security, and on the other claims a value-laden approach to foreign policy —an approach that conceals amoral maneuvering based mainly on narrow, short-run self-interest. The loose piety of political appeals to God and country has had its counterpart in the self-righteous crusades that have sought to establish American interests abroad in the guise of spreading and defending democracy.

At the same time, our means have often contaminated our prime values. The cynicism and opportunism that embraced Franco, that failed to take a strong stand in the United Nations against an anachronistic colonialism, that avoided significant action against South Africa, that would use almost any military means to win victory in Southeast Asia, that permitted the creation of a secret CIA army in Laos—these cannot defend themselves with an appeal to liberty and equality. Thus the pragmatic approach to foreign policy has at the same time subverted our most enduring principles and weakened American prestige and power. In short, it does not work. It is *un*realistic.

ENDS VERSUS MEANS

The dualism in American foreign policymaking goes back far into our history. The realists who shaped our posture toward other nations during the first half century—men like Washington, Monroe, the two Adamses—for the most part understood the relation between our specific ends—above all, sheer survival on a continent occupied by foreign powers—and the limited means they had to work with. Later in the century, as the nation became more secure, more isolated from European quarrels, and more expansionist, American statesmen turned various policies and expedients into moralisms and pieties. Free trade, protection, isolationism, imperialism, a big navy, disarmament, and other means variously became ends in themselves.

All this was not of global significance during much of the nineteenth century, but by the end of the century the United States was emerging as a world power. To a great degree, Theodore Roosevelt reverted to the strategy of early statesmen. Operating with force and shrewdness in foreign affairs, he was able to intervene vigorously in the Japanese-Russian conflict and adroitly to lower tension among the Great Powers over Morocco. But recognizing the limits of American power, he also knew when *not* to intervene. When he was urged to act on behalf of Jews in

Russia and Armenians in Turkey, he answered that it was a literal, physical impossibility to interfere in such cases, save in the most guarded manner, under penalty of making the nation ridiculous and of aggravating instead of ameliorating the fate of those for whom America would interfere.

But this same Roosevelt was also a moralist and a preacher who was not above bullying smaller nations and intervening in the affairs of Latin American nations such as Santo Domingo. In both foreign and domestic affairs he spoke frequently of his ends —justice, honor, responsibility—but these often lacked substance and bordered on the purely symbolic or ritualistic. According to Harbaugh, he acted in foreign affairs "with impetuosity and restraint, with bluster and sensitivity, with belligerence and accommodation." Almost all his actions were accompanied by high-blown and righteous self-moralizing, but whether morality was the prime motive for the action, or whether the action was simply rationalized by pieties, was usually unclear. The wielder of the big stick, ironically, was also a recipient of the Nobel Peace Prize.

On the face of it, no such dualism characterized Woodrow Wilson. He seemed to be the supreme moralist. He came to Washington with a complete set of ethical values in domestic affairs— values he had little trouble extending to American policy and preaching for the whole globe. He believed, as Sidney Warren has noted, that a nation was a "moral essence" that should be guided by the same standards of moral conduct as applied to individuals—even though, of course, individuals were ruled by governments and nations were ruled by no one. During his first term he acted as a kind of preceptor for the world, lecturing other nations—especially Latin American nations—as to how they should behave. His sense of mission and righteousness rose to a pitch with the advent of war. "Our object now, as then," he declared in his war message of April 1917, "is to vindicate the principles of peace and justice in the life of the world as against selfish and autocratic power and to set up amongst the really free and self-governed peoples of the world such a concert of purpose and of action as will henceforth insure the observance of those principles. . . . The world must be made safe for democracy."

But Wilson could practice realpolitik too. Finding at length that the Mexicans would not adopt the kind of "righteous" government he believed in, he followed a hard policy toward their new leaders. He sent Marines into Haiti, the Dominican Republic, and Cuba; in fact, says Warren, Wilson's administration conducted more interventions than had been undertaken by both Roosevelt and Taft. On the other hand, he followed a conciliatory policy toward Colombia, actually proposing to apologize for Roosevelt's "petty larceny" of the Panama Canal zone. The problem was not that Wilson was variously a moralist and a realist; the problem was that, despite his rhetoric, he had no overarching hierarchy of ends that permitted him coherently to marshal his means. Thus his deepest commitment through his whole life seemed to be to individual liberty, and the war was fought against an autocracy that was supposed to be trampling liberty, but both during the war and after it Wilson directed or permitted a series of federal actions that were a fundamental departure from the Bill of Rights.

Perhaps it was not surprising that Franklin Roosevelt, a boyhood admirer and distant cousin of Theodore Roosevelt, and later an activist in the Wilson administration, should have embraced both morality and realpolitik, but here again the issue was not following both courses of action but the relation between practice and purpose. I concluded, in a study of Roosevelt in World War II, that the critical point was "less Roosevelt's simple separation of political ends and military means than his capacity to marshal his means of all kinds—military, institutional, propagandistic, diplomatic, and indeed political—in support of his most fundamental objectives. His failures lay in linking the ends and the means. Thus, he was banking on Soviet popular as well as governmental confidence in the willingness of the Big Four to share and sacrifice together, yet he agreed to a long delay in the cross-channel attack. He wished to recognize the potential role of the several hundred million Chinese people but made Chung-

king a poor third in the allocation of military assistance, and he
was unwilling to apply the political pressure that was the only
conceivable way to bring about military and possibly political
and economic reforms in China. He was deeply concerned about
colonialism and expressed strong views to the British about India
in particular, only to draw back when Anglo-American cooperation seemed threatened. . . .

"Roosevelt was a practical man who proceeded now boldly,
now cautiously, step by step toward immediate ends. He was also
a dreamer and sermonizer who spelled out lofty goals and sum-
moned people to follow him. He was both a Soldier of the Faith,
battling with his warrior comrades for an ideology of peace and
freedom, and a Prince of the State, protecting the interests of his
nation in a tumultuous and impious world. His difficulty lay in
the relation between the two. The fact that his faith was more a
set of attitudes than a firmly grounded moral code, that it embraced hope verging on utopianism and sentiment bordering on
sentimentality, that it was heavily moralistic, to the point, at least
in the view of some, of being hypocritical and sanctimonious—all
this made his credo evocative but also soft and pasty, so that it
crumbled easily under the press of harsh policy alternatives and
military decision."

It was not only that Roosevelt's lofty dreams and his practical
compromises were inconsistent with each other; they also over-
emphasized the importance of each other, for the loftier he set
his ends and the lower he pitched his practical compromises, the
more he raised men's expectations while failing to fulfill them.
How this gap was closed depended on postwar policy. And, on
this score, Roosevelt had left a rich inheritance. The defeat of
Hitler had been crucial to the defense of liberty. And whatever
the inconsistencies in his basic strategy, he had invented a host
of specific policies and techniques that would be fruitful in the
postwar world, at the same time that he had expressed his ideals
unforgettably in his Four Freedoms, his call to Americans to be
citizens of the world and members of the human community,
and his rejection of "the system of unilateral action, the exclusive

alliances, the spheres of influence, the balances of power, and all the other expedients that have been tried for centuries—and have always failed." Roosevelt had also helped shape promising arrangements: a new world organization and machinery for vast economic and military aid to allied nations, but the world organization was to have limited authority and was subject to a big power veto, and it was hampered by an intricate system of precisely the kinds of spheres of influence and balances of power that Roosevelt had spurned in his rhetorical appeal.

So eloquently had the failing leader put forth his ideals and so receptive had the people been to them that one might have expected the nation to be locked after the war into a fervent, messianic crusade for world freedom, international altruism, and collective security. In fact almost the opposite happened. As the cold war succeeded the big war, as fear replaced confidence as the motivating force in foreign policy, and as the ground shifted under their feet, policymakers reverted to concepts and policies that mirrored the old "expedients." Their policies became ambivalent and disjunctive. The United States built up and employed a tremendous military force, including nuclear weapons, though it made sporadic efforts to disarm; it fostered spheres of influence and balances of power in some areas while helping establish collective regional and hemispheric policies elsewhere; it intervened with military power in Korea and Cuba and Vietnam, but not in Hungary or the Suez or Czechoslovakia; it acted multilaterally in some dangerous international situations and unilaterally in others; it gave economic and military aid to some nations and withheld it from others; it retaliated against "provocative" incidents in some instances (the Gulf of Tonkin) but not in others (Pueblo incident); it lied piously on some occasions (the U-2 incident) and was disarmingly frank on others; it gave strong support to the United Nations but retained its power of unilateral action.

Policymakers had given up certain naïve assumptions about the ways of power in the world, but they had not found a way to reconcile their stated ends with means applied. We had overcome a series of myths that I summarized in an earlier volume: "the myth of American omnipotence and the myth first of Soviet incompetence and then of Soviet invincibility; the myth that utopian gestures of ours such as unilateral disarmament will be followed by equally benevolent actions on the part of other powers; the myth that economic aid and democratic indoctrination automatically influence developing nations toward democratic ways and the myth that they never can; the myth that some one instrument of national policy, such as nuclear weapons or free trade or humanitarianism or ideological warfare or pacifism or international organization or brinksmanship or neutrality or balance of power, will, if pursued long enough and hard enough, bring about a resolution of our difficulties abroad." We were more sophisticated, more wary. Despite complaints that we looked on communism as monolithic, in fact Washington dealt quite differently with the governments of Russia, China, Rumania, and Yugoslavia.

How explain this burst of principled realism? In part it was recognition of the essential fact that as ends must determine means, available means also condition ends. It became clear after the war that the United Nations was not, in any way, a world government, and that policies of containment and balance of power, which seemed to offer the same old status quo to people yearning for liberty and equality, simply acknowledged that power was still fragmented among nations. Any attempt to overthrow the balance of power would call for such force, and unleash a war of such universal devastation, as to cause destruction far worse, by any benevolent measure of human value, than the maintenance of the balance of power. In part the postwar principled realism recognized the revolution in weapons of war. Statesmen earlier had been able to accept war—even terribly costly world war—as acceptable means to the goal of national security and survival. Technology changed this. Nuclear war would so threaten belligerent nations, and innocent ones, that unleashing such war would be an almost suicidal act, conceivable only if a nation faced imminent invasion and destruction. Nuclear war might quite literally obliterate the goal of survival itself. In this context, "better red than dead" is at least arguable, though, for many, life on such terms is equivalent to moral death. But in this situation, such slogans would have little value. Flexible strategies, wide options, sudden shifts of policy, continual compromise and adjustment and accommodation, become, if not moral means, at least defensible and perhaps even indispensable.

VIETNAM: THE REVERSION TO DOGMA

After twenty years of the most eclectic and versatile combinations of policy within the fragmented global context, of flexible initiatives and responses (behind a smog of Dulles rhetoric), how did we get mired in a protracted, cruel, and totally frustrating war in Indochina? Mainly it was the elevation of expedients and contrivances into dogma; it was the transformation of means *into* ends.

One dogma was the overreliance on the sphere-of-influence conception itself. South Vietnam was on our side of the bamboo curtain. The line of partition at the seventeenth parallel had somewhat limited legitimacy, but we clung to it as if it were the Canadian-American border. As a general concept the sphere of influence was of course fundamental to our whole postwar strategy, as we had demonstrated in shoring up Western Europe, Greece, and Turkey militarily and economically, and in *not* intervening in Hungary and Poland and Czechoslovakia. But making a fetish of any particular border was a different matter. Willingness to negotiate over territory is crucial to any kind of lasting sphere-of-interest strategy.

Another dogma, ironically, was the conclusion that limited warfare could be won. The gradual escalation in Vietnam contrasted significantly with the strategy in Korea. In the earlier crisis we had moved speedily and powerfully and with UN backing. The whole effort was a brilliant success until we appeared to be threatening China's borders. To be sure, the naked aggression of the North Koreans had made a full and quick response much easier for the United States than did the slow political subversion in Vietnam later, and the memory of China's riposte in North Korea also inhibited our strategy in Vietnam. Still, the decision to help South Vietnam but not to invade or massively attack North Vietnam forced Washington to operate within narrow strategic margins. "As soon as the United States took over the main function of the war in 1965," as Theodore Draper has said, "it condemned itself to fighting either an unlimited war from the outset —and horrifying the world and its own people—or fighting a 'limited war' which it could not win without exceeding the limits that would make the other side fight an unlimited war. This is the contradiction which the theorists of 'limited war' never thought through." Rigid incrementalism failed.

The Russians sometimes do better, pursuing policies of limited war but not dogmatically, as means not as ends. They seem to know when to mass overwhelming power. There was something ludicrous in 1968 when the Soviets and their satellite regimes moved an enormous weight of men and armor into a hapless, helpless Czechoslovakia. But Moscow seemed to know what it was doing, at least from the perspective of retaining Soviet dominance over restless European satellites. It took no chances that the situation would get out of hand. Its generals must take some satisfaction in comparing what they accomplished in Bohemia with what the Pentagon accomplished in Vietnam. With hindsight it has been argued that Washington would have done better in Vietnam if it had followed a Korea strategy—if it had invaded North Vietnam and then negotiated a settlement guaranteeing the existing border between the two Vietnams. But the Chinese might not have cooperated. And the American people, to whom invasion is a dangerous weapon of policy, would doubtless have reacted with intense disapproval.

The immoderate moderation of American policy, the rigid adherence to a middle-of-the-road course that is often the most dangerous way to travel, stems from a commonsense devotion to consensus. And trying once again to follow a middle course between falsely conceived extremes proved our undoing. Because Vietnam encompassed most of what everyone wanted to do, concluded Leslie H. Gelb, director of Defense Department policy planning and arms control during 1967–1969 and a leader of the group that wrote the secret study based on the "Pentagon Papers," because it was "the basis of consensus, it was full of contradictions, the consequences of which were disastrous for our Vietnam policy. We tried both to bomb more and to negotiate seriously, even though bombing prevented negotiations. We wanted the South Vietnamese to do more of the fighting and at the same time we wanted a larger direct combat role for ourselves, despite the fact that the latter gave the South Vietnamese the perfect excuse not to do the former. We sought both to reform the Saigon government and to give the Saigon leaders whatever they asked for, thus leaving ourselves without any leverage. The result was a hodgepodge that could not work."

A third dogma was the faith in military gimmickry. Certainly in no other war did so many assurances leak out that some new military tactic or gadget would turn the tide. As usual it was the airmen, with new innovations in bombing or attacking, who took the lead in this old charade. Public relations men sought to sell search-and-destroy, hold-and-protect, trip-wire defense systems, electronic listening devices, and various theories of counterinsurgency as though they were cure-alls. As the gadgets and nostrums repeatedly failed and the military forecasts went awry, credibility steadily eroded. By 1968, when the generals claimed that they had won a military victory in the Tet offensive, people just did not believe them.

The elevation of these and other means into dogmas—virtually into ends in themselves—was not the only source of the failure in Vietnam. The absolute determination of the communists, Hanoi's backing by Moscow and Peking, the geography of the area, the lack of American expertise in Indochina, the weakness and corruption of the various regimes in Saigon—these and other factors were important. Given such inevitable difficulties, the question in foreign policy, as in domestic, is how to intervene effectively by finding a point of leverage among opposing forces. The United States, a fertile incubator of dogmas in foreign policy, became a prisoner of them.

Overemphasis on military techniques meant underemphasis on political methods. The United States never brought the compelling pressure to reform on Saigon that might have generated a long-run rejuvenation of the South Vietnamese polity. Another possible political solution was repartition of South Vietnam as the basis of a settlement with Hanoi. As the war progressed it became clear that the seventeenth parallel, unlike most of the lines that had been drawn or confirmed following World War II, badly reflected the political and military realities of Vietnam. Geneva, in 1954, simply confirmed the old territorial settlement. A new partition, granting Hanoi parts of the northern, upland, and inland areas of South Vietnam, much of which it already dominated politically and ideologically, could have given Hanoi, in contrast to Nixon's Vietnamization policy, a quid pro quo for a ceasefire. But Washington never squarely confronted the possibilities and problems in such a political alternative, and hence the people did not.

The lesson of Vietnam and our other misadventures is that an effective foreign policy in a constantly changing world calls for endless new combinations of policy. Addiction to any one means is perilous. Success of a particular doctrine or technique in one situation or in one decade does not guarantee that it will work in the next. Certain procedures, institutions, or arrangements of course have more reliability and fixity than others. Given the world of separate sovereign states we live in, certain means—the balance of power, spheres of interest, techniques and traditions of diplomacy—will be more dependable than others. But even these old arrangements have so often failed in the past, and are so vulnerable to the rush of technological and political change in this century, that they too must be coolly appraised and selectively employed.

VIETNAMIZATION: THE NIXON GAMBLE

The withdrawal from Vietnam appeared to show Nixon at his most skillfully manipulative. Vietnamization provided him with an ideal middle way between pressures from those who wished all troops out by a date early and certain and those who wanted a continuing American presence, as in Korea. Pulling his forces out in contingents of a few thousand at a time, announcing grand totals at politically advantageous moments, soothing public opinion with promises of more, stretching out the whole process to give Saigon more time to prepare its forces, Nixon was able for more than a year after Cambodia to keep public opinion—and the demonstrators—from engulfing him.

Skillful—yet terribly risky. The basic rationale for our ten years of intervention in Indochina had been the incapacity of the noncommunist South Vietnamese to defend their country against the communists. But there was little indication, as the Americans withdrew, that they could do so in the future without allied military backing. Hanoi's successful counterattack against the Laos invasion and subsequent communist successes elsewhere in Indochina were a clear warning that the North Vietnamese could still achieve the goal that the Americans had denied them.

A decisive military setback in Vietnam would doubtless bring a political upheaval at home. Hanoi could hardly forget that its most telling feat in the last few years had not been victory on the battlefield but its own military failure—or at best a military stand-off—which had ended up as a stunning political victory over the Americans. This was the Tet offensive of 1968. Even while the isolated and beleaguered communist forces were trying to recover from the counterattacks on them, the Johnson administration was quivering under a blast of criticism from those who felt betrayed by the repeated promises and predictions of an early victory. Lyndon Johnson soon after announced his retirement. The Tet offensive more than any other incident brought a decisive turning point in American attitudes toward the war.

Would Hanoi repeat this kind of strategy? Much depended on its estimate of Nixon's political plans. Communists have learned to follow the making and remaking of presidents as avidly as Americans do. A sudden shattering attack against the South Vietnamese from the north or west, or a well-timed, intensive, escalating campaign of armed subversion throughout the country—or a combination of both—could leave Nixon's Vietnamization policy in ruins and produce an abdication by the president or his defeat in the fall. What would Hanoi learn from its president-watching? Presumably it would fear above all the reelection of President Nixon, for that would put into the White House for another four years, without any hope or worry about reelection, a man whose only fundamental value, publicly expressed, is a brand of anti-communism, 1950s style. On the other hand, the president-watchers in Hanoi might calculate that a newly elected Democratic president, no matter how committed against the war in his preelection promises, might revert to the old "imperialist-colonial-aggressive" line. Or Hanoi might simply conclude that American presidential politics was beyond calculation and pursue its own tactics on its own continent.

Still it was altogether possible that Nixon might just get away with it—that he might enter the election campaign period with almost all Americans out and with South Vietnam still intact. But a successful gambit for Nixon personally could mean a greater risk for the country, for it would be achieved only by postponing the resolution of the underlying problems. At best he might help bequeath to Indochina an endless, spreading civil war, with incalculable casualties. At worst he might help bequeath such a war followed by a communist victory and the loss of everything that 45,000 dead American soldiers had been told they were fighting for. All this would doubtless bring on an agonizing period of political tumult and reprisal during the mid-1970s.

For Nixon's strategy in Indochina had two fatal flaws. One was his escalation of means over ends—his continuing promise to get all Americans out of Vietnam without making clear even the military implications of this action. Rarely had an administration committed itself so flatly to a specific foreign goal and to success as Nixon did on Vietnam—hence rarely had an administration been so vulnerable to domestic or foreign threat to that commitment. Second, the administration had not confronted the political implications of Vietnamization. It assumed that somehow Hanoi would be willing to let the Americans leave and then desist from subversion and aggression in South Vietnam—as though North Vietnam could quit without achieving the aims for which *its* tens of thousands of men have fought and died for twenty years, against French and Americans.

Nixon's effort at rapprochement with China immensely increased the gamble in Vietnam. He played up his visit so enthusiastically that he aroused people's expectations and, hence, made any failure all the more of a letdown. He also gave Peking a tremendous advantage, for the Chinese could cancel discussions or repudiate understandings without any fear of popular disapproval. This unequal leverage between Washington and Peking would enable the latter to use its advantage to threaten Vietnamization. Faced with a combination of military pressure from North Vietnam and diplomatic blackmail from China, Nixon could be forced into the tightest political corner he had ever known. The danger was not so much of collapse under pressure but erratic behavior, jerks and twitches rather than a steady handling of crisis. In his farewell talk to the president and cabinet Daniel P. Moynihan had warned against "lurching from crisis to crisis with the attention span of a five-year-old." Much depended on Nixon's ability to conduct the kind of rigorous self-analysis that, for all his self-appraisals, he had never accomplished, and on his capacity to fix a course of action, to assert moral authority, and to set grand strategy rather than one more tactical improvisation.

THE NEW DOGMAS

One might have hoped that the dogmatism that helped mire us in Vietnam would have proved to be so calamitous that a more adaptable foreign policy would have now superseded it. Alas, the old cure-alls and panaceas such as bombing or the domino theory continue to dominate. But there has emerged in the aftermath of Vietnam a congeries of reflex dogmatisms that may fix the compass of our foreign policy in a new but equally rigid position.

When the final balance sheet of the Vietnam tragedy is struck, doves as well as hawks will have to bear their share of the blame for the substitution of means for ends. In the earlier years of the conflict it was the doves who were absolutely convinced that if the administration would only adopt this device or that, the war would soon be over. The placards that they paraded before the White House in those days reflected their certainties; those placards demanded that the president end the bombing, promise no invasion of North Vietnam, "NEGOTIATE NOW." As it happened, all three admonitions were tried out and all three failed. The other dogma—coalition government of communists and noncommunists, preceded or followed by elections jointly conducted by them—was not tried. If it had been, doubtless we would have discovered again what long experience and sound theory tell us—it is virtually impossible for communists and noncommunists to share real power in gaining popular backing or in running a government, at least in a deeply divided, strategically located nation. At any rate, it was not the invalidity of the doves' dogmas, but the fanaticism and rigidity with which they were put forward, that helped produce the inflexibility in American policy.

The great danger now is that the recoil to Vietnam will produce reflex dogmas as rigidly confining as the shibboleths of the hawks. For example:

1. The *anti*-domino dogma. From the shibboleth that communist "conquest" of one nation meant automatically that neighboring countries would fall to the reds, whether in the East or the West, whether to the Russians or to the Chinese, whether by subversion or by open onslaught, we have moved half circle to the gospel that dominoes *never* fall. The very metaphor of the falling dominoes must be one of the most unfortunate similes

ever inflicted on the task of thinking about American foreign policy. The idea that the defeat or collapse of one country automatically knocked down a neighboring one has itself fallen like one of the dominoes. By the late 1960s, even to mention the term before a knowledgeable audience was to invoke jeers or mirthless chuckles.

But to move to the contrary notion—the notion that countries can "fall" without *any* effect on neighboring countries—is of course equally absurd. In fact, conquest or collapse of a regime can have profound implications for a whole region or hemisphere. Certainly this was the case with the coming to power of communist regimes in Russia, East Europe, China, Cuba. Just what effect such events have is a matter not for catechism but for the most complex diplomatic, military, and psychological analysis. "There is no question that there was *some* validity in the dominoes simile," Adam Ulam summed it up. "But life, politics, and history do not follow such neatly worked out theories and analogies." Chess or bridge would be a more useful simile than dominoes, if game theory is relevant at all.

The anti-domino dogma was part of a more dangerous shibboleth. This was the anti-containment theory. Under Secretary of State Dulles the United States had seemed to embark on a crusade, at least rhetorically, to put a finger—or a fleet—into every breach through which the red hordes might flood to devour good Christians. Under Kennedy and Johnson—indeed, under Eisenhower himself—the policy of containment was actually quite selective, but still containment became a bad word. Yet intelligent containment by noncommunist nations of communist, and by communist nations of noncommunist, sustains the present balance-of-power, sphere-of-interest system by which the world stumbles along with some show of equilibrium. It is one thing to feel, as George Kennan does, that containment has been badly or at least indiscriminately applied. It is something else—and quite absurd— to say that containment never works. It is much like saying that operations for cancer always work, or never do. Yet this kind of thinking has become commonplace not only among the New Left but among liberal editors who write about the "archaic doctrine" of containing communism.

2. The anti-patriotism dogma. "Our country, right or wrong" has been replaced by "My adversary, right or wrong." Those who seize on every misdeed and excess of Americans in Indochina and elsewhere, and these are easy to find, often fail to criticize those of, say, the communists or the military dictatorships of the developing nations. The rising criticism of American foreign policy ends and means has been a salutary development on the whole, but if communist citizens cannot openly protest against their own governments' actions and if foreign critics refuse to, freedom as an end everywhere in the world assumes a lesser priority than the correction of America's acknowledged and unacknowledged sins —a correction that is, in my view, only a proximate goal toward the ultimate purpose of freedom and equality among all men.

3. The no-monolith dogma. This is the theory that communist nations do not act in a concerted way abroad, whereas America and its allies always do, and that communist societies are marked by diversity and pluralism at home, whereas America is dominated by conformity. All this is a reaction against years of official propaganda about the red peril, the communist network, the Comintern's or Cominform's plots against Western democracies, combined with the growing perception of conformity at home. Certainly the picture of monolithic communism was extreme, and the American self-image naïve. More and more evidence suggests that most of the major initiatives of individual communist as of many noncommunist governments since World War II were taken unilaterally. Even the secondary or tertiary communist nations such as East Germany or North Vietnam are perfectly capable of action on their own.

But the new dogma that communist nations rarely, if ever, act in concert in major political confrontations, and that the split between China and Russia is the ultimate disproof of monolithism, is equally at odds with the evidence. In a crucially important respect the communist nations *have* been acting in concert. However unilateral the original action, the communists have managed to stick together in any subsequent showdown. This was the case in Korea; Moscow is believed to have sponsored the invasion of South Korea in 1950 but Peking came to Pyongyang's (and its own) defense. Both Russia and China have given military and economic aid to Hanoi. Moscow directed the invasion of Czechoslovakia but was supported by Poles and Hungarians and other satellites. There *is* a concert of communist defensive power, as there tends to be among noncommunist powers, even if the Soviet bloc, like the western nations, produces internal strains and divergences.

The companion theory of internal liberalization of communist societies has had a history of its own. Repeatedly during the Soviet state's fifty years of unchallenged power westerners thought they discerned technological, economic, and ideological developments that seemed to be making for a convergence between communist and noncommunist societies. The increasingly overt projection of dissent and criticism among intellectual and artistic groups and among the young in communist countries seemed especially promising. Ulam concludes that "it would be mistaken to assume that the dissent is widespread, that the enlightened ideas of a Sakharov, the passion for telling the truth about the Soviet past and present of a Solzhenitsyn, can now or in the near future be *openly* supported by a sizable segment even of the educated class." We must distinguish between ferment within small intellectual and artistic enclaves and open dissatisfaction among wider groups of managers and workers. The latter exhibit few signs of serving as material for liberalization. Not one of the 738 signatories of Russian letters protesting against various trials, according to Robert Conquest, were from the managerial group. For a time under Khrushchev it did seem possible that Soviet society as a whole was headed toward convergence. But the Kremlin's hard internal line of recent years reminds us that a people saturated for years in antiliberal, antilibertarian, anti-

western propaganda are not likely to generate pressures toward
reform and liberalism. This is at least as true in China. Those
expecting results from Ping-Pong diplomacy and other openings
to the West must reckon with the enormous saturation impact of
indoctrination on a whole generation of Chinese. We must not
permit ourselves a new romanticism about China at the same time
that we uproot romanticism about America.

4. The anti-presidential power dogma. The 1970s, like the
1770s and many periods in between, have brought a reaction
against executive power. Since the president was the chief initiator of the Vietnam war, and since most of the governmental opposition has developed in Congress, it was only natural that
people would look for some way to restrict the presidential warmaking power. Two caveats are in order. Congress is not necessarily a restraint on the president at times of crisis; on the contrary, historically Congress has often been the chief source of
interventionism, adventurism, and even jingoism. It is only some
time later when the venture goes sour that Congress plays up its
cautious, restrictive role. Second, no legislature can provide the
steadiness, the restraint on the military and the activists, the timing, the concerted action, the consistency of policy that can at
least be hoped for from the executive. It is not by chance that no
major western democracy conducts its foreign policy through its
legislative branch, or even gives the legislature much of a veto
power. The advice that Hans Morgenthau directed successively
to the Eisenhower, Kennedy, and Johnson administrations, while
perhaps too sharp to be wholly palatable today, is still essentially
sound:

"It is for the President to reassert his historic role as both the
initiator of policy and the awakener of public opinion. It is true
that only a strong, wise, and shrewd President can marshal to the
support of wise policies the strength and wisdom latent in that
slumbering giant—American public opinion. Yet while it is true
that great men have rarely been elected President of the United
States, it is upon that greatness, which is the greatness of the

people personified, that the United States, from Washington to Franklin D. Roosevelt, has had to rely in the conduct of its foreign affairs. It is upon that greatness that Western Civilization must rely for its survival."

LINKING ENDS AND MEANS

It is not hard for a people to embark on a grand crusade in pursuit of their ideology throughout the world. Nor is it hard for leaders to follow a cautious policy of realpolitik. What is hard is the course that the American people must pursue—to maintain its faith in democratic goals of liberty and equality, to encourage their protection and realization throughout the world, to work vigorously toward their realization at home—and to realize that it does not possess the means of creating them in other nations. Limited means can diminish our strategy of realizing human ends without diminishing either our conviction that in the long run these ends must win out for the great majority of mankind—or our efforts to do what we can with the limited instruments we have.

To explore the ways in which America's ideals have been blunted or subverted or denied in domestic and foreign policy is to consider ways in which means may become more consistent with ends in a time of rapidly accelerating change. To do this adequately, it is necessary to acknowledge in foreign policy, as in domestic policy, the extent to which means have failed. The pragmatic approach to foreign policy has not only made possible the unexamined reliance upon dogma but the rejection of dogma where useful—as in the avoidance of response in the suppression of freedom in Czechoslovakia. It has justified support of dictators when convenient. It has rationalized military intervention where U.S. interests were threatened. It has sanctioned the virtual destruction of a country on the ground that such means—from defoliation to forced migration to Mylai—were necessary or inevitable methods to save that country from a fate worse than death. Indochina has been the epitome of the tragic and blind transmutation of means into ends, the logical result of a foreign policy that has not sorted out proximate goals and ultimate goals, that has not attempted to maintain consistency between means and deeply held national values. The disaffection of the young, their sense of outrage and national betrayal, and the profound unease of the nation as a whole are the logical consequences. World War II had national support because, generally speaking, the ends were consistent with democratic values. Korea tormented the nation because it seemed, at first, consistent with justifiable ends, but, as the war extended toward China, less supportable. Vietnam has devastated the nation because the limited goals of power were transformed into massive violence that brought deadlock and dishonor, hence losing support of both pragmatists and idealists. It is a failure of both ends and means.

It is also a failure of human purpose. In his State of the Union address in 1971 President Nixon warned with Emerson that "things are in the saddle, and ride mankind." But events, including major developments abroad, can be mastered only by a comprehensive, systematically conducted political strategy, as was attempted in World War II or in postwar Europe, not by rigid military tactics, fuzzy foreign policy doctrines, or eye-catching public relations schemes. Nixon himself was almost a caricature of the expediency of previous presidents. He had become a manager-in-chief who had developed little of Franklin Roosevelt's or John Kennedy's feel for the grain of history, nor had he found inner or outer guidelines for judging and mastering events. Whether mankind would be ridden by things, or things by mankind, in the 1970s would turn on a creative union of means and ends that would go far beyond the small triumphs of practicality and public relations.

CHAPTER **4**

Overturning the System

Millions of young Americans reject the system because they believe it is beyond salvation. Its arteries have hardened so that blood cannot flow through any more. They see the voting process as mere game-playing, freedom of the press as a charade, civil liberties as therapeutic devices that conceal from the people the sources of their real oppression. Work, in this system, is mere exploitation and the nine-to-five working day in vast bureaucracies a long indoctrination in conformity. Patriotism, asserting a superiority that the nation is unworthy to claim, is a farce. Racism is so embedded in the national consciousness that no gradual means can root it out. The nation is essentially evil and the evil can be exorcised only by turning the system upside down.

The young revolutionaries reject not only the system but the ideas that rationalize it. While they speak of distorted priorities and corrupted principles, in effect they are responding to the derangement of ends and means that has characterized so much of the nation's life. While they share with most Americans an ultimate belief in such values as liberty and equality, the difference is, they say, that they really mean it. Hence they would substitute a whole new set of human, political, and institutional means to realize their heartfelt ends. Is it possible that revolu-

tionaries—using the term in its generic sense as meaning the overthrow of the existing system and the establishment of a new one—
have solved the age-old dilemma of the countless nonrevolutionaries who have become hopelessly entangled in their ends and
means? Or is it possible that the very habits of American thought
that have dominated the realistic, practical men in power have
also diminished the capacity of revolutionaries to reason out the
interrelation of their own ends and means—that they, too, have
been corrupted by the gospel of "what works"?

Certainly the most impressive aspect of the revolt of the young
has been their capacity to act. They have voted with their feet
against foreign and domestic policies; they have issued revolutionary manifestos, occupied deans' offices, marched on the Pentagon, disrupted classes, thrown a convention city into turmoil, and
in some instances fired and bombed buildings. To thousands of
students, blacks, and women, revolution has become a serious,
a deadly business.

Some dismiss the revolutionaries and protesters and rioters as
small bands of terrorists (generally, white) or as dangerous militants (generally, black). "What would dead American revolutionaries of the 1770s have said to this charge?" asks Carl Oglesby.
"Did you never hear what we did to our own loyalists? Or about
the thousands of rich American Tories who fled for their lives to
Canada? And as for popular support, do you not know that we
had less than one-third of our people with us? That, in fact, the
colony of New York recruited more troops for the British than
for the revolution?"

Others deal with revolutionaries by psychoanalyzing them.
". . . They hate themselves so much," Bruno Bettelheim exclaimed
to William Braden. "And they are so unable to make a go in this
world that they feel the only way they can make a go in this
world is by destroying it, so the cares in the external world will
be comparable with the cares in the inner world." Negative identity? he was asked. "That's right. So you see to me, as a psycho-
analyst, their behavior is an extreme defense maneuver to avoid

a total, a complete break with reality. If I cannot manage reality as it is, either I can change myself—that's hard work—or I can try to change reality in my image. Which is exactly what a paranoiac is trying to do, whether he's called Hitler or by any other name."

Kenneth Keniston has a different theory. After investigating the views of some New Left activists who participated in the 1967 Vietnam Summer protest he concluded that these young persons had already resolved what is normally considered as the adolescent crisis. They had a sense of inner identity; they knew who they were and what they were good at; they had shown an ability to succeed and excel in conventional fields; they had come to terms with their sexuality; and they were capable of meaningful relationships with other people. They had become *psychological adults*. But they were *sociological adolescents*. They rarely had spouses or children. They could work hard but they avoided occupational commitments. They remained "deliberately uninvolved with the institutions, guilds, and organizations of their society."

But phenomena cannot be dispensed with by explaining their causes. And revolutionaries have seldom seemed to be safe, stable, adjusted, or really happy people. Even the rather genteel American revolutionaries of 1776 did not seem very nice by reputation to the English gentleman. And today's young revolutionists have an easy answer to the Bettelheims: "If we are full of self-hate it is a direct product of the corrupt American system—and one more good reason to change it." No, character analysis has never stopped revolutions or revolutionaries. The need is for social analysis.

REVOLUTION—DO THEY MEAN IT?

Revolution has become, for most who use it today, another sponge word. It was never very precise; witness the easy use of the terms industrial, scientific, social, or literary revolution. When

President Nixon can term a reorganization of government spending "the new American revolution," something has happened to
a once glorious word. Or consider Charles Reich's "revolution"
of Consciousness III, which reveals itself as a matter of music,
clothing, food, and the like. Only later will the political structure
—laws, institutions, and social structure—be altered "in conse-
quence." It is not explained how or why, after the revolution of
beads, soul food, and rock has been won, there is any need to
accomplish a new, hardier, and grubbier transformation. One
need only THINK REVOLUTION to accomplish it. Whether in the
New Left or Women's Liberation, the raising-of-consciousness
approach appears only to set the stage for fundamental changes;
it may be, in fact, only the secular version of the evangelical
gospel that insists on the conversion of the multitudes as a precondition for social salvation. It has its uses as individual therapy
and does awaken many to recognize the bars that imprison them,
but it is a long, slow, and essentially gradualist route to genuine
social change. Although their goals may be quite different, the
means of these radicals are similar to those of conservatives who
claim that social change and morality cannot be legislated, that
change must take place first in the private, divided heart. But
there is considerable evidence that, in fact, institutional change
can lead to a change in behavior, and the latter to a change in
attitudes, as seems to have been happening to a marked degree
in the South since the *Brown* decision.

"Consciousness" revolution is only a happening. It is the kind
of revolution even nonrevolutionaries like to participate in or, at
least, observe. It is gay, colorful, loving, soul-full. But it is not in
earnest. It is revolution for the hell of it. "Just what the students
on the left would most like to be—revolutionaries—that is just
what they are not," says Hannah Arendt. "Nor are they organized
as revolutionaries; they have no inkling of what power means,
and if power were lying in the street and they knew it was lying
there, they are certainly the last to stoop down and pick it up. . . ."

What then is a serious revolution? As I use the term here, it is the use of violence and other extra-constitutional means and the fundamental transformation of economic, social, and political institutions in order to effect *actual* social change that realizes the values of the revolutionaries. It is to go outside the system in order to change it, on the theory that to use the processes of the system is to be trapped within it.

To be serious about revolution is to be serious about both its ends and its means. As to ends, one must really "mean it"—and understand the ramifications of what one means. One must want not merely social change over the long run but relatively rapid, deep-lying transformations in men's lives and institutions—how they live, what goods they get, what values they realize, the rules they live by, the power relations between man and government and between man and man. Revolution ultimately goes beyond even this; it determines how people think, what they see, what they want, what they expect. Serious revolution deals with the whole man and it is, therefore, both exciting and dangerous. Because it may do this with verve and style, it attracts romantics even when it has no lasting place for them.

To undertake such a revolution is the most portentous political decision a man can make. Some Americans made it during the 1960s. It is easy to dismiss revolution as impossible in America, but the events of the past decade have taken the word *impossible* out of our political dictionaries. To serious revolutionaries attention must now be paid.

The essential logic of revolution—and its great attraction to many rational people—is its powerful effort to link ends and means, that is, to grasp the implications of ends for the means seen necessary to realize those ends, and of means for the possibility and desirability of achieving those ends. The crucial question of means is the extent to which the revolutionary is willing to use violence, and what kind of violence, to realize revolutionary goals. Since the means are always implicated in the ends, the decision for violence goes to the heart of what the revolution is all about. Among other things the revolutionary must assess correctly the system he is rebelling against. To what extent does it allow nonviolent techniques that could serve revolutionary goals—such techniques as sit-ins, marches, boycotts, rent strikes, nonviolent civil disobedience, passive resistance, and other devices of "creative disorder"?

Of course the violent revolutionary faces a terrible dilemma on this score. The more a society seems to provide peaceful methods of change—protection of free speech and assembly, the right to vote, and all the rest—the more the revolutionary must rationalize the use of coercive tactics that bypass those methods of change. Hence he must demonstrate that television is not really open and accessible but monopolized by reactionary corporate overlords, that the press is controlled by its advertisers, that free speech is a defensive device for the bourgeois rather than a positive tool for the poor, that tolerance is a liberal cliché—in short, that the Bill of Rights is either meaningless or is choked off at the point where it can really be used against the oppressors. The revolutionary must also deal with claims that indeed the mass media have given enormous exposure—many would say overexposure—to revolutionary protest and disarray, that the press remains open to a variety of views and above all to news that reinforces conflicting opinions, that today, in fact, a man can utter the most flammatory words without realistic fear of governmental reprisal.

It is not necessary here to dwell on this old controversy. The key question is the extent to which revolutionaries *analyze* the society against which they are rebelling, the extent to which they can bring the morality inherent in their own goals to bear on the means they propose to adopt. And it must be said that revolutionary thought in America has been highly deficient on this score. Of many examples, let me cite one. In 1970 Robert Coles conducted an "underground dialogue" with Father Daniel Berrigan shortly before the priest was arrested. Among other things Coles was interested in the ethics of revolutionary violence—a matter to which a theologian in Father Berrigan's position presumably would have given considerable thought.

What about violence and hate and brutishness in the underground itself? asked Coles. Why were the Weathermen in any better moral position than members of the Ku Klux Klan?

"Well," said Father Berrigan, "I look upon the Weathermen as a very different phenomenon because I have seen in them very different resources and purposes. I believe that their violent rhythm was induced by the violence of society itself—and only after they struggled for a long time to be nonviolent. I don't think we can expect young people, passionate young people, to be indefinitely nonviolent when *every* pressure put on them is one of violence—which I think describes the insanity of our society. And I can excuse the violence of those people as a temporary thing. I don't see a hardened, long-term ideological violence operating as in the case of the Klansmen."

Coles pressed him on the matter. Was he not getting close to the position of Herbert Marcuse and others?—"you feel that *you* have the right to decide what to 'understand' and by implication be tolerant of, even approve, and what to condemn strongly or call 'dangerous' at a given historical moment. You feel *you* have a right to judge what is a long-term historical trend, and what isn't, and you are also judging one form of violence as temporary and perhaps cathartic and useful or certainly understandable, with the passions not necessarily being condoned, whereas another form of violence you rule out as automatically ideological . . . ?"

"O.K.," Father Berrigan answered. "Well, let's agree to differ on that, maybe from the point of view of a certain risk that I am willing to take in regard to those young people—a risk that I would be much less willing to take in regard to something as long-term and as formidable as the Klan. But I am willing to say that there is always danger in taking these risks, and that the only way in which I can keep free of that danger, reasonably free of it, is by saying in public and to myself that the Weatherman ideology (for instance) is going to meet up with people who are going to be very harshly and severely critical of it, as I have been and will be; in fact, at the point in which their rhetoric expresses disregard of human life and human dignity, I stand aside and I say no, as I will say no to the war machine. But I discern changes in our radical youth, including the Weathermen. And again, I have hope for them, hope they will not be wedded to violence."

Could any reasonable person studying this exchange and the rest of the interview conclude that Father Berrigan was demonstrating anything but a derangement of values on the pressing question of violence? He expressed his personal opposition to violence and stood aside from it but presented to Coles every defense of violence in special situations. He saw a distinction between Ku Klux Klan violence and Weathermen violence—a distinction evidently not convincing to Coles and certainly not to this reader. He saw *every* pressure being put on young people toward violence—this in a world of loose family structures, permissive teachers, sexual freedom, enclaves of privacy, student demonstration, sit-ins, marches, and every other kind of protest. He saw violence by the young as a temporary thing when history shows that violence begets violence. He excused youthful violence on the ground of violence in the oppressive society—which means that revolutionaries would be borrowing their oppressors' end and means in fashioning their own. And he contented himself with the thought that the Weathermen would not continue to indulge in violence because they would encounter persons who would condemn violence harshly and severely, but Father Berrigan himself was not willing—at least in this interview—flatly to *condemn* violence.

The argument against violence as a conscious instrument of social change is not simply based on corruption of good ends through adoption of contradictory means, but also a practical one of long-run consequences. Just as nuclear war has become too perilous a means to serve as an option in the strategies of power, so domestic violence in a complex, fragile society could unleash such demons that the benevolent ends alleged to be sought could be swallowed up in chaos. In such a disrupted society, where no law is binding, justice withers. This is a condition that breeds fascism, not democracy. Violence in the service of a majority— as in a guerrilla movement or in combat against an army of occupation—may be effective in achieving goals. But violence in the service of a minority whose power is less than that of the majority is almost always doomed, unless the minority can appeal to the highest values of the majority. Violence has been employed in America chiefly *against* liberal and radical change rather than in its behalf—as slaves, union workers, blacks, and young people can attest.

All this makes it the more curious that so many American revolutionaries, who fairly batten off existing civil liberties in receiving protection for their writings and in their deeds, denigrate liberty both as a means of bringing about change and as an end of the revolution itself. The intellectual godfather of many American revolutionaries, Herbert Marcuse, has been quite candid about his willingness to withdraw the right of free speech from those with whom he differs. If the way of a submerged but rising majority of the people is blocked, he has said, its reopening "may require apparently undemocratic means. They would include the withdrawal of toleration of speech and assembly from groups and movements which promote aggressive policies, armament, chauvinism, discrimination on the grounds of race and religion, or which oppose the extension of public services, social security, medical care, etc." Since Marcuse would deny liberty to his adversaries, those who believe in the principle of individual liberty would, as a practical matter, be sorely tempted to deny Marcuse the right to use free speech and assembly in his effort to realize his views. But this, of course, is what the principled civil libertarian will not do; he, unlike Marcuse, will not be "practical" in restricting his adversaries because he knows the dire implications of this kind of "practical" means for his ultimate ends.

Presumably Marcuse is subordinating civil liberties as a means to some transcendent end; it is interesting to contemplate what end he would place above civil liberties in whatever utopia he espouses. But all this is to assume that modern revolutionary thinkers in America have worked out a structure of ends, proximate ends, and means that are relevant both to the way power would be gained and how it would be exercised. But evidently they have not. Rather, they have subordinated the most precious value a democracy can embody—individual liberty—to some end that they cannot or will not define even to the people who are supposed to commit themselves to it.

REVOLUTION: WHAT ENDS?

But if revolutionaries have been cloudy or confused about means, they are vague to the point of being cryptic about their ends. This is not just an American phenomenon; Califano found that revolutionary students in many other countries admitted to having no immediate goals at all and were not sure of what kind of society they wanted.

Revolutionary talk deals mainly with indictments of the entire existing society; to a lesser degree it deals with immediate, short-run tactics of violence and nonviolence; and it hardly deals at all with the nature of the society that would be substituted and just how it would bring about real social change in desired directions.

These infrequent statements of goals, furthermore, tend to alternate between the immediate and superficial on the one hand and the remote and utopian on the other. Thus the Berkeley Liberation Committee's program of June 1969, aimed at setting a "revolutionary example throughout the world," offers thirteen points: "We will make Telegraph Avenue and the South Campus a strategic free territory for evolution . . . create our revolutionary culture everywhere . . . turn the schools into training grounds for liberation . . . destroy the university unless it serves the people . . . struggle for the full liberation of women . . . take communal responsibility for basic human needs . . . protect and expand our drug culture . . . break the power of the landlords and provide beautiful housing for everyone . . . tax the corporations, not the working people . . . defend ourselves against law and order . . . create a soulful socialism in Berkeley . . . create a people's government . . . unite with other movements throughout the world to destroy this racist capitalistic imperialist system." So, too, some of the black power militants have set forth demands for reparations and programs comprising a collage of immediate concerns and long-range purposes that combine the rational with the irrational. The Black Power manifesto originally promulgated by Charles Forman in a demonstration at Riverside Church presented issues similar to the Berkeley revolutionary document.

Soulful socialism! To the extent that revolutionaries are not willing to clarify the criteria for their ends they are following a self-authenticating revolutionary morality, as the theologian Richard Neuhaus has called it—a morality that cannot be judged by standards outside the revolution. Neuhaus quotes Andrew Kopkind: "Morality, like politics, starts at the barrel of the gun." Ends are swallowed by the means.

Revolution, Neuhaus insists, must be only the means of last resort. He sets out severe tests of the right of revolution. It must be in defense of basic popular rights, which must be in real jeopardy from the existing regime. Nonviolent means of social reform must have been exhausted. The existing regime must have lost its moral authority. The revolutionaries must be motivated by good intentions, defined not as purity of personal motive but seriousness of political program or goal. Only moral means must be used. And there must be reasonable hope of success, at not too high a cost in injury suffered.

Revolution, in short, is a serious business—far more serious than the revolutionaries in America seem to recognize. If they were serious they would subject themselves to the discipline of hard thought. To sloganeer about power to the people and romantic socialism—or any other kind of socialism—is to evade the trying questions of just what a people and their government will do with their power. In just what concrete ways will "people power" change things, working through or reshaping what procedures and institutions, overriding whose interests, altering which structures in what ways, and—above all—in terms of what values fully conceived and marshaled. The lack of a rational approach to such stated purposes may lead to inversion of means, as, for example, when Roy Innis, rhetorically one of the most militant of blacks, moved on to deals with white southern governors for reinforced segregation. Because the revolutionary sentiments in this country do not embody that kind of thought they take on a mindless and even banal quality.

And a blatantly undemocratic one, for a creed that appeals to popular catchwords and symbols. The great rationale of the system against which revolutionaries rebel is that it provides a fair and dependable process for steady change—the process of majority rule and minority rights. Revolutionaries contend that civil liberties—the Bill of Rights and the right to vote—are simply historic expressions and current instruments of bourgeois power. By ignoring the use of civil liberties by socialists, labor, farmers, populists, and other minorities to make changes in the system over the whole course of American history, revolutionaries can repudiate majority rule on the ground that majority rule has no legitimacy except in a context of minority rights. From all this it is an easy step to the argument that the great mass of people are bamboozled by the capitalists and their minions who control the media and hence the revolution must be conducted over the heads of the masses it serves.

Even if one argues against these grounds for the moral right of revolution, however, one must concede that the right *has* existed for various groups throughout almost all of American history. The right to revolt has been held successively by Americans who were not effectively represented in the English Parliament in the eighteenth century; by men who, lacking a certain amount of property, could not vote under the new Constitution; by slaves; by women until the passage of the Nineteenth Amendment; by Negroes, especially in the South; and perhaps by eighteen-to-twenty-year-olds, until their recent enfranchisement.

A BLACK REVOLUTION?

If any group still retains a moral right of revolution, it is, of course, the American blacks. That moral right may be shrinking as Negroes win the vote in the South and elect throughout the country a dozen members of Congress and hosts of state legislators, city councilmen, and board of education members, but the residue of oppression is heavy enough to provide considerable justification for blacks who reject the existing "white" system. Many see a choice of only two basic strategies—separatism or revolution. The separatists have been notably vague as to just what kind of separatism they want—whether in local communities, in an apartheid region in the United States, or in Africa. In 1967 a Black Power Conference in Newark resolved "that the Black Power Conference initiate a national conference on the desirability of partitioning the U.S. into two separate and independent nations, one to be a homeland for white and the other to be a homeland for black Americans." Such a plan not only left a few questions open; it departed from a venerable Negro ideal, proclaimed by Marcus Garvey and others, to recross the Atlantic and establish an African empire. Doubtless it is a mistake, however, for whites to view such proposals operationally; they are in large part today, as in the past, means of demonstrating the blacks' own desperation and their hatred of white society rather than a serious movement to break out of the system. "There comes a time," the Negro leader James Weldon Johnson said many years ago, "when the most persistent integrationist becomes an isolationist, when he curses the white world and consigns it to hell." But Johnson was never a separatist.

For four decades after the Russian Revolution Negro leaders showed little interest in the American Communist party, but, in the 1960s, some turned to the banner of revolution provided it was colored black rather than red. "We must move from resistance to aggression, from revolt to revolution," proclaimed H. Rap Brown. "For every Huey Newton, there must be ten dead racist cops, and for every Black Death there must be a Dien Bien Phu. May the deaths of '68 signal the beginning of the end of this country." But black revolutionaries share one trait with white ones—an incapacity to define their goals, except in the haziest terms, or even to work out tactics that might serve their ends. They cannot escape the grim paradox that has confronted most revolutions in this country and abroad—they must work with human materials unpromising for revolution, that is, with the blacks who will not risk their precarious economic, social, and psychological footholds in the existing society for a dangerous leap into the unknown.

However, despite the label "black militants" and other inflammatory epithets used against them, most of those who took part in ghetto riots have been persons caught up in the explosion of feeling and behavior, burning and looting, not as a calculated ideological tactic—in contrast with the Weathermen's manufacture of bombs—but as a spontaneous, contagious expression of previously suppressed rage. This is the fuel of revolt; indeed, young blacks refer to the riots as rebellions. But it is not a strategy of revolution. It does not rationalize means or articulate ends; it simply *is*.

But for those who are consciously revolutionary, an obvious tactic would seem to be a black-white coalition against the system, and white revolutionaries have been eager for this. The black leaders will not accept coalition; their goals are different and their racist rage is too strong. "We don't see SDS as being so revolutionary," said David Hilliard, chief of staff of the Black Panther party. "We see SDS as just being another pacification front that's given credit by the fascist establishment in order to cause disfusion in hopes that this would weaken the support for the Black Panther party . . . we'll beat those little sissies, those little schoolboys' ass if they don't try to straighten up their politics. . . ." However, if blacks cannot ally with radical students, to what other group can they turn? But blacks, among themselves, have not been in agreement on this strategy, and some of the most militant have promoted coalitions with white radicals.

All this is not to underrate the significance of the Black Panthers and similar groups on their own terms. Some of them may, of course, be merely Black Power versions of old street gangs, with the same hierarchy of leaders and the same punitive methods against traitors though now more politicized and ideological. But many are college students or dropouts (almost all their casualties in the 1968 Chicago police raid were either in or just out of college), well informed, passionately concerned for the deprived, willing to do beneficial things like serving breakfasts to children. Adolescent, sometimes hustlers, often melodramatic, they are generally nonviolent in practice despite their rhetoric, resorting to guns and fists mainly in self-defense. But their good works have little to do with a strategy to gain power and in fact may militate against it.

Still, the public spotlight on the black militant rhetoric has obscured the fact many young blacks are organizing in the South and in the northern cities to form disciplined political cadres to work within the system but to attempt to transform it in basic ways. The differences between the behavior of a number of white middle and upper class youth and black middle and upper class youth are instructive in this regard. At Columbia University, in the unrest of the late 1960s, black and white students had separate campus headquarters, not only for reasons of racial identity, though this was part of it, but also because blacks regarded white students as too undisciplined to serve their own goals. Whites combined a permissive style of life and contempt for property with their political tactics; blacks collected garbage, policed their quarters and arranged with adult political finesse to evacuate their building in a dignified order. A number of this same black generation is now engaged in zealous political activity in both North and South while many of their white compatriots moved out of the system into communes and enclaves abroad or into the drug scene. The young black youths had seen drugs destroy many in the ghetto; like the Black Muslims, they had opted for disciplined commitment to political process—and this required the suppression or at least redirection of an anger that could have been dissipated in self-destruction (an anger that has, indeed, destroyed others, such as George Jackson of the Soledad Brothers). The frustration of such affirmative efforts—which, like the efforts of their parents in the basically rational civil rights movement, rest on a faith in America—could lead to dangerous consequences not only for the blacks in America but for the society as a whole.

These young blacks like the leaders of the civil rights movement reject both separatism and revolution as a sufficient tactic, whatever their emotional identity with such movements, and call for a third strategy—one that would seek to transform the whole system, including its politics. They take the rhetoric of America seriously but they believe that American practice is so sterile and hypocritical that basic changes in power alignments must be brought about if the rhetoric is to become a reality. Perhaps, as a group, they believe in their dream more profoundly than any other group in America.

Other groups besides the blacks have their revolutionary fringes, that is, factions or movements that propose to operate outside the system as they define it. There are those women liberationists who believe they cannot attain equality with men until the whole structure of male chauvinism is overthrown. There are the poor who have been organized by blacks or students or others who have seen a revolutionary potential in the poverty-stricken, although on the whole these groups have operated within the system, organizing in a labor union, as Chavez's followers did, or in a reformist group, as the Welfare Rights Movement has. There are the tens of thousands of people who have sought to escape traditional society by joining the three thousand communes currently estimated to be going concerns in the United

States. There are those intellectuals who have chosen to go their way outside the customary channels—though most of these accept salaries from traditional universities. And there are the anarchist and nihilistic groups that reject any organized government at all.

Granted the heroic, compassionate, and creative potential in all these groups and their organizers, those who operate outside the system cannot be regarded as serious political revolutionaries by the standards advanced here. They do not have a considered plan for gaining power. They do not have a definite program for wielding power. They have worked out a variety of day-to-day tactics and they have developed a vocabulary of rhetoric, but nothing—no strategy of action, no plan of governance—links their immediate means and their foggy ideology. Essentially they are not revolutionaries in earnest because they are not relevant to the processes of real social change.

In stating why a new radicalism should be anti-ideological, Howard Zinn has, in effect, explained why revolution in America has not been serious. A new radicalism, says Zinn, "should be—and here it has been inadequate—concerned with theory. I see three essential ingredients in such a theory. First we need a vision of what we are working toward—one based on transcendental human needs and not limited by the reality we are so far stuck with. Second, this theory should analyze the present reality, not through the prism of old, fixed categories, but rather with an awareness of the unique here and now of the need to make the present irrationality intelligible to those around us. Finally, such a theory would explore—in the midst of action—effective techniques of social change for the particular circumstances we find at the moment." No one has better stated the way in which revolution has *not* gone about its business in America.

Why have American revolutionaries, in contrast with, say, Russian ones, failed so markedly to think through the interrelation of their ends and means? In part because the recent revolutionary movement, among whites, has coincided with the war in Vietnam, opposition to which has been the heart and soul of white radicalism since 1965. The entire thrust of the New Left in recent years, some of its leaders point out, has been to stop the war in Southeast Asia. The war has acted as a powerful catalyst in the building and expansion of the movement; yet the urgency of this all-consuming immediate goal of ending the Vietnam war has forced a preoccupation with short-run tactics of resistance to the virtual exclusion of the broadening of the movement and the development of a long-term revolutionary program, and it has further polarized white and black radicals, for whom the consuming issue is not Vietnam (though they tend to agree with the judgment against it) but the achievement of racial justice. The failure of the Black Power movement has been due, in part, to its focus on rhetoric and its lack of attention to a coherent philosophy and program of ends and means. Actually, the most vigorous systematic thinkers among blacks calling for fundamental social changes have not been labeled militants but have operated within the system.

All this is not to dismiss the importance of individual revolutionary leaders and activities. But these have been important, essentially, in episodic and spasmodic influence on the system from within, in the same manner as any reformer or reform group, or in goading and defying and jarring the system from without. In either case the essential influence of the revolutionary is exerted within the parameters of the existing system. His role is essentially no different from that of the radical or the liberal. And every time he spurs and shocks the system toward a little movement and progress, he lessens by the same measure his chances of overthrowing the existing system and establishing a new one. The great revolutionaries, such as Lenin, recognized this predicament.

The implications of all this for the liberal or radical American who is working within the system are equally serious. The more he comprehends that revolution against the system cannot succeed in America, the more he must face up to the failure of his own strategy.

Part II

✿

THE PRACTICALITY
OF PRINCIPLE

CHAPTER 5

The Mobilization of Change

Neither piecemeal change nor violent revolution—neither working through the system nor overturning it—can overcome deep-seated, tightly interlocked, and long-persisting problems in America. Neither incrementalism nor revolution goes to the heart of the matter; neither, despite its rhetoric and its compassionate intentions, is a serious attempt to confront the actual social behaviors, attitudes, and institutions that determine the processes of change. To be serious does, of course, call for concern and for action, but it also calls for dimensions of thought and action that neither gradualism nor revolution can satisfy.

Purposeful change requires hard thought. First, factors that block imperatively needed social change must be analyzed and strategies must be explored to overcome the blockage. Second, the ends we wish to achieve must be defined and understood. Unless we can think through both these dimensions of uncommon sense, the course of social change will have neither theoretical substance nor long-run practical effect. Change will be erratic in its direction and defiant of social control. We will continue to be the victim of events.

One of the most appealing qualities of Americans—or so well-disposed foreigners tell us—is our ability to roll up our sleeves, spit on our hands, and take on a practical job. Doing a job can mean fighting a brush fire, repairing a neighbor's wind-damaged home, helping children of migratory workers in a nearby town, coordinating regional transportation, harnessing a river valley, beating Hitler, building an atomic bomb, landing a man on the moon. In recent decades the nation has seemed to commit itself to certain demanding jobs of social change—abolishing poverty, ensuring decent health and nutrition and housing, gaining control of the environment, suppressing crime and violence, easing the crisis of the cities. Given our reputation for solving problems, one would expect to report accelerating progress.

Merely to list these big jobs, however, is to feel a sharp pang of failure. We have noted how the men of affairs, after two centuries of compromising over civil rights issues, found that the problem had not been solved, and the black man would wait no longer; the effort to overcome poverty is an equally compelling example of the unworkability of "common sense" approaches. The most practical of men—businessmen, politicians, bureaucrats, realistic reformers—have been "fighting poverty" for at least a century. The job of stimulating the economy was largely left to big business in the last century; they claimed that the free enterprise system would guarantee substantial prosperity if only it was unrestrained, and we took their word for it. In this century abolishing poverty has become a public concern. Presidents such as Wilson, Hoover, and the two Roosevelts, Truman and his successors, have addressed themselves to the problem of "poverty amid abundance." Business and industry have been drafted as allies. Scholars have prepared analyses of causes and formulas for remedy. Commissions have been appointed, reports rendered, laws passed, funds allocated, people hired, charity handed out, job training established, welfare granted, public works built, social security broadened, job corps set up. Almost everything seems to have been done, in short, except abolishing poverty.

In recent decades, especially, the abolition of poverty has been a conscious programmatic goal, rather than just part of the American dream or heritage, or just a by-product of business success. Franklin Roosevelt dramatized the problem of one-third of the nation ill-housed, ill-clad, and ill-nourished. He advanced an economic bill of rights and Congress passed an employment act. Truman retained his office in 1948 largely on the basis of his promise to deal with the economic problems of the poorer workers, farmers, and Negroes. Poverty was at the top of John Kennedy's domestic agenda. Lyndon Johnson declared war on it —unconditional war. Nixon acknowledged its pressure and offered welfare reform. Yet poverty persists in gross form. It has been alleviated; a number of people have moved out of poverty; some of the scattered efforts have had measurable effect. But the results are minuscule in relation to the money and effort spent. As in urban public education where student achievement declines as budgets mount, poverty does not seem to respond to money alone.

The cause of the problem cannot be simply lack of economic resources or technology or concern or even political commitment. The cause must lie somewhere else. Is it possible that practical men have failed essentially because they have failed to define the dimensions of the problem? I do not mean the usual kind of definition and reflection—eyeing the job, calculating the tools and materials and time needed, rounding these up, and getting to it. I mean seeing the job in the widest context of what produced the problem in the first place, how it relates to other problems, whether it can be solved without dealing with related situations. This means more than being radical in the usual sense of "getting to the root of things." It means getting to the root of the problem—that is, its entrenchment in a social context—and also seeing the implications of "doing a job" for attitudes, interests, and institutions that operate in the broader context of the problem. It means a rational strategy in the fullest sense.

Consider what happens when we set out to do an ordinary job. First we must agree that the problem exists and that a job is called for and possible. If one man undertakes a small job on his own, he must calculate other persons' reactions, including the supposed beneficiary. If groups are involved, a consensus is required, at least among leadership. Then men pitch in and "do" the job. The house is repaired, the stream cleaned up, the children given food and clothes, metropolitan transportation drawn under one governmental structure, the Tennessee Valley Authority established and empowered, and so on. The problem is solved. What has happened can typically be described as piecemeal change, improvement, or reform.

Some problems can, indeed, be overcome by such discrete, segregated action. The house may be repaired, the brush fire put out. Even big jobs can be done. But accomplishing the big jobs is usually done by isolating a whole series of actions from the wider society as much as possible. Thus landing men on the moon called for establishing an autonomous environment—separate compounds, facilities, budgets, personnel, motivations, controls—so that space efforts would not be enmeshed with routine domestic problems. The same happened at Los Alamos, where a separate society was created to build and test the atomic bomb. Or in a climate of emergency and hope a TVA is established; its effectiveness and durability are reinforced by decisions to protect it as somewhat autonomous from the broader society and government, so that it will have its own environment in its own valley. The Marshall Plan was carried out by semiautonomous agencies operating outside the usual governmental channels. Each of these efforts is a compelling instance of how government *can* bring about change under certain conditions; each was successful in its own way because it dealt with an isolable problem and rallied funds, authority, and public support to the end in view.

THE IRON GRIP OF HISTORY

But very few deep-seated, persistent, and widely influential problems are susceptible of this kind of segregation. They are entangled with a host of other social situations and hence:

1. The more entrenched and widespread the problem and the more vigorous, persistent, and comprehensive the reform action, the more the action tends to activate new sets of attitudes that may not have been part of the original consensus supporting reform. Thus efforts to help the migratory workers' children evoke both supportive and resistant actions from the parents of the children, farmers, government agencies, farmworker organizers. (Of course one could simply bestow food and clothing as the Ladies Bountiful did Thanksgiving turkeys on the doorsteps of the poor, but even this seemingly innocuous action may alter expectations.) The basic political tendency is to "widen the community of the concerned." Concern about what? Concerns are varied and multitudinous. The decisive question is the nature of the attitudes that may be evoked. They may be agreeable to the consensus supporting the original impetus to "do a job." But in a pluralistic situation they are just as likely to evoke hostile or inhibiting passive attitudes in the wider community.

2. Not only does the widening effect of "piecemeal reform" run into crosscutting attitudes and motivations. It runs into a web of ultimately resistant social relations and processes. This web is composed of existing family, neighborhood, community, and wider private and public agencies and linkages that reflect the equilibrium of the status quo. Any powerful and persisting reform effort threatening that equilibrium, no matter how benevolent in motive, is likely eventually to encounter "veto groups" that can limit the impact of the proposed change. These veto groups may be formal or informal, open or covert, but they operate to slow down and sometimes to suffocate the force and effect of the thrust of a single, narrowly conceived change.

If the consensus for reform is wide and deep enough, lasting change in institutions and attitudes may occur. But, typically, a major reform effort provokes resistance from unexpected sources. These may be a church group, a teachers' union, a taxpayers' association, and they will manifest their influence directly through the circuits of information and opinion and, more formally, through public agencies. The larger the community, the more variegated, unpredictable, and resistant these forces are likely to be.

Let us pitch the problem on a broad, national level. Years ago Richard H. Tawney wrote an arresting book, *Equality*, in which he pictured poverty and deprivation in Britain not as a kind of manifestation or happening or aberration, nor even as "natural" or "inherited." Inequality, he said, was a combination of social organization and class attitudes. Inequality was *made*. It was a product of the manner in which property, education, the legal system, medical services, and other social opportunities and powers were organized and distributed. Inequality was a congealing of status, ideology, and power. Tawney found not only the obvious pyramid of wealth but a hierarchy of opportunity, a near-monolith of life chances and deprivations. The dignity of a man turned on arbitrary distinctions of birth, money, health, schooling, connections, speech. Poverty was created by the system and validated by the ideology, which was part of the system. Tawney felt that a similar system of economic inequality in America might be tempered by tendencies toward social equality and opportunity. But, as he wryly noted, a right to the pursuit of happiness is not the same as the right to attain it.

What Tawney put into a structural framework we can put into a historical or linear form. "From the moment of birth," Robert Lynd wrote, "the accidents of cultural status—for instance, whether one is born 'north or south of the tracks'—begin to play up and to play down the potentialities of each person. As life progresses, culture writes cumulating differences recklessly into these individual lives. . . ." Applying this proposition to individuals, one might consider the southern Negro child born into and imprisoned by a familiar set of circumstances—a shabby tenant farmer's home, coercive landlord-tenant relations, no political influence within the community or outside, wretched schooling, lack of medical facilities, invincible segregation, crippling speech habits, and above all, feeble hopes and expectations. Only a decisive event could upset this equilibrium. But let us assume that such an event does intervene, such as a world war. A job opportunity suddenly summons from Chicago or Detroit; the family makes the long trek north. But the new broader environment may not open up. On the contrary, the old vicious cycle reasserts itself—shabby home, ghetto life, poor schooling. . . . The family finds itself in a new prison, a prison in many ways perversely like the old.

Historians sometimes refer to the "cunning of history." Better to talk about the iron grip of certain processes of history, since we cannot assume some central intelligence or design. A stream of events combines to keep that black family locked into a ghetto prison. The coming of the slave ships, plantation life in the South, civil war and emancipation, continued segregation and suppression, the breakout, the re-creation of the structure of deprivation in the North. Some believe that a *conspiracy* of history accomplished the imprisonment; others would doubt that any group of bourgeois or colonialists or whites could plan or carry out such a vast undertaking. Does it matter whether the imprisoning events were a conspiracy or merely a concatenation? Not to that black family, perhaps. Giant forces must have been at work, whether centrally directed or not, to fix its destiny with such an exquisite set of controls.

How that structure of inequality was erected, what modifies, erodes, or transforms such a structure, how history writes cumulating differences into men's lives, how history can be modified —these are both cosmic and immediate questions. Would it be possible for history, or for a structure of power, to write cumulating *equalities* into men's lives as it has written in inequalities?

We are no longer talking about "practical" problems. These are highly theoretical questions—questions of social causation to which social scientists and historians devote their professional lives. They are matters not of common but of uncommon sense. The commonsense questions were settled long ago. *These* are questions that demand of us hard and rigorous thought about the

interrelation of long, tangled chains of events and complex structures of interaction and about our own capacity to break those
chains and to restructure our society.

THE THEORY OF CUMULATION

In 1944 Gunnar Myrdal, at the conclusion of his *An American
Dilemma,* presented a note on the "principle of cumulation."
Earlier he had described the Negroes' "poverty, ignorance, super-
stition, slum dwellings, health deficiencies, dirty appearance,
disorderly conduct, bad odor and criminality" as stimulating and
feeding white prejudice against them; the white prejudice in turn
kept down the Negro plane of living, so that an equilibrium was
created between the caste situation and the prejudice. It was a
dynamic equilibrium in that if the plane of living was lowered
or white prejudice rose, a mutual interaction supporting a tighter
caste system was created between the variables, ad infinitum.
But cumulation could work in the opposite direction—stimulated,
for example, by a "gift from a philanthropist." The "vicious circle"
could work either way—toward a caste system or toward breaking it up. All of this, of course, was grossly oversimplified—but
the simplification was complex enough.

From this kind of reasoning Myrdal drew his hypothesis for his
principle of cumulation: "If, in actual social life, the dynamics
of the causal relations between the various factors in the Negro
problem should correspond to our hypotheses, then—assuming
again, for the sake of simplicity, an initially static state of balanced forces—*any change in any one of these factors, independent of the way in which it is brought about, will, by the aggregate
weight of the cumulative effects running back and forth between
them all, start the whole system moving* in one direction or the
other as the case may be, with a speed depending upon the original push and the functions of causal interrelation within the
system."

One trouble with this formulation was the simple matter of

italics. By emphasizing the part of the formula that he did, Myrdal gave the impression that any one significant "push" impinging on a structure in equilibrium would be enough to start a process of cumulative change. But his own investigations—and those of many others—of the actual history of the Negro in America had demonstrated that one push had never been enough. For more than a century the most practical reformers, blacks and whites, northerners and southerners, had been advancing single solutions to the Negro "problem." Slavery, emancipation, segregation, migration abroad, separatism at home, trade-union organization of blacks, black capitalism, political organization, philanthropy, more education, better health care, job training, migration to cities, integration, radical social or political action, coalition with whites—all these and a host of other plans or tactics had been advanced as commonsense solutions to the situation. Myrdal's own description of Negro progress by the early 1940s attested to the substantial failure of all these practical reforms. During the past century slavery had been abolished, some suffering had been alleviated, some blacks had made advances, many had been freed from tenant-farmer imprisonment—but the essential Negro "problem" remained. Indeed, by emphasizing the eventual impact of any single change, Myrdal was in effect supporting a theory of gradualism or incrementalism that did not square with his own findings or his own radical perspective.

What saved the hypothesis and gave it immensely greater theoretical sweep and significance were the unitalicized words: ". . . with a speed depending upon the original push and the functions of causal interrelation within the system." The functions of causal interrelation could work either way. They could stall and stifle the reform impetus, as we have noted above, because of the array of negative or hostile attitudes and veto groups and institutions. By the same analysis they could stimulate them. If one wished to effect a speedy and comprehensive change in a rooted social structure, he must seek to bring about changes in a *decisive number of the causal forces* so that the *cumulative effects would immensely reinforce one another and transform the whole structure.* Instead of linear, piecemeal, and episodic efforts over a long period of time, the reformer could try carefully interrelated efforts all across the line during a much shorter period. No single reform action could possibly do the job. A series of powerful, well-coordinated "pushes" presumably could.

All this might seem rather obvious, a matter of common sense. If so, it is not the kind of common sense that has been acted on. Indeed, it is ignored so often that it must be relegated to the category of uncommon sense. Thus, recently, certain public figures concerned about poverty came up with a truly breathtaking idea. People were poor? That meant that they did not have enough money. Simple. Give them money. But imagination, if not experience, should tell us that giving money is not enough—that in a condition of poverty, joblessness, lack of schooling, poor health, lack of motivation, and all the rest, handing out money has heavy costs as well as benefits, and in any event is no long-term solution to the problem. The lack of money is only one of the foundations of the edifice of poverty.

As one moves from piecemeal reform to comprehensive reform the difficulties caused by working through much more complex institutions and challenging a much wider array of veto groups increase at an almost geometrical rate. Deciding on a new school building, for example, raises questions of taxes, location, and design; these can be flammable issues but are usually resolvable because the type of decision and the channels of change are familiar, restricted, and manageable. Building a new school *system* raises not only these several questions but even more controversial issues of social class, neighborhood patterns, segregation and integration, busing, teacher accountability, state and federal aid. Reconstructing or reforming an entire metropolitan structure adds further questions of transportation, industrial plant subsidy and location, zoning, federal-state-local relationships, environmental development, protection, and control, and other "quality of life" as well as "quantitative" issues. At the national level the difficulty may be even greater. "The more ambitious our goals in terms of full employment," as Charles Schultze points out, "the more we must sacrifice goals of price stability and balance of payment equilibrium. Programs that seek to raise farm prices and incomes conflict with the objective of lower consumer prices. The goal of reducing traffic accidents conflicts with the desire for rapid transportation and widespread car ownership. The goal of efficient urban transportation often conflicts with aesthetic values and values associated with displacing low-income residents. Altruistic values are an important part of the political process, and professional cynics are unrealistic in denying their existence. Nevertheless, altruistic values conflict among themselves as well as with self-interest values."

THE GREAT ENTANGLEMENTS

Even thorny and complicated issues such as these, however, dwindle in complexity compared to the stupendous domestic problems this book is mainly concerned with—poverty, race, the cities, the environment. For these problems cut across every sector of the society and the economy. Evidence on this score became overwhelming toward the end of the 1960s. In 1967 President Johnson's National Advisory Commission on Rural Poverty, in its report *The People Left Behind,* made it clear that urban poverty and rural poverty were inseparable—the urban riots of 1967 had their roots in the rural poverty of the previous decades. To deal with rural poverty, the commission made clear, meant to deal with illiteracy, ill health, bad housing, decline of rural communities, shrinking tax bases, poor local government, and a host of related situations. Rural America had a culture of deprivation that rivaled Tawney's structure of poverty.

A year later the Advisory Commission on Intergovernmental Relations, in its report *Urban and Rural America: Policies for Future Growth,* also underlined the interrelation of the urban and the rural crisis of poverty and deprivation. This report, for example, raised the question of stopping or slowing migration to the city—an action that would send shock waves through the whole structure of American government. This commission, too, stressed the interlocking of a multitude of factors. Statewide programs of urban development should include measures such as land banks, land and development rights purchase, new community building programs, urban renewal, housing, highway construction, state parks, air and water pollution, water conservation, health facilities. Federal policy in the area of mobility and migration alone would embrace such questions as resettlement allowances; on-the-job training allowances; interarea job placement; elimination or reduction in the "migrational pull" of interstate variations in public assistance eligibility; strengthening federal-state programs of family planning; federal assistance in large-scale community development. The eye runs rapidly over these bureaucratic, jargon-filled terms; but those concerned with their implementation will immediately understand the explosive social and political issues that any such serious effort would create.

In the last few weeks of President Johnson's administration, the National Commission on Urban Problems submitted to the Congress and to the President a report on *Building the American City*, commonly called the Douglas report after the chairman of the commission, former Senator Paul H. Douglas. Here, again, a commission that had begun examining one general issue found that that issue ramified into every nook of the society and the polity. The commission went further and held that "government had long addressed itself to the separate components of the urban experience"—unemployment, deteriorating housing, segregation, crime, disease—but only in the past decade "have we developed a sense of the effect of all of these forces working together in the modern metropolis." The commission made scores of recommendations calling not only for action by national, state, and local government but for the closest articulation of them.

Other investigations have had much the same experience. To uncover one serious problem is to see its close involvement with others. Thus the National Advisory Commission on Civil Disorders found that at the core of the riots was not a single cause but race discrimination, economic deprivation, family disorganization, personal insecurity, consumer exploitation, residential segregation, the black migration from the South, and the white migration to the suburbs. To meet the ghetto's grievances, the commission recommended that employment be increased through the expansion of training programs, consolidation of recruitment efforts, creation of more jobs, development of underdeveloped regions, fostering of ghetto enterprise. Education should be attracting better teachers, developing new curricula, reducing class size, improving preschool and precollege programs. Welfare should be reformed, housing upgraded—and so on.

Of all the problems that pose the need for concerted governmental efforts, however, the crisis of the environment may prove the most complex. Nature simply does not recognize the practical boundaries man has built around his piecemeal efforts to deal with his environment. The fragmented organization of man has dramatically encountered the balance and order and unity of nature. A typical "ecological platform" covered such items as abortion; birth control; land use for scenic, recreation, or open-space purposes; ocean shoreline development; curbing the tax loopholes that favor land speculation; logging restrictions in national forests; regional and basin-wide development programs; ecological education; severance taxes on mineral extractions; reuse of containers; a moratorium on large-scale technological projects; higher taxation of bigger cars; overhauling of farm subsidies.

The environmental crisis also forced a new awareness not only that government must do these kinds of things but that it must do them with a control and coordination that is unprecedented in the administration of our domestic affairs. The environment has shown itself supremely resistant to efforts at piecemeal change; many of such efforts had simply exacerbated the problem. To build highways, or to destroy pests, or to develop a recreation area, or to plan economic development, or to foster ribbon development of housing, without understanding the interrelation of such activities in a delicately balanced environment is to court not only failure in one's specific efforts but environmental disaster. In short, we will need the same massive and concerted intervention for environmental protection as is required to save our cities and to attack poverty and racism at their roots.

To conclude that planned social change can take place only through coordinated control of change in a variety of channels is to glimpse the formidable nature of any major effort at reform. It means that power must be mobilized across a broad political, economic, and social front in order to stimulate and carry through vast changes. It implies that institutions must be reconstructed in order to permit and accelerate such changes. It assumes rare qualities of political leadership. These issues will be the burden of the last three chapters of this book. We must deal first with the implications of the argument so far: in moving from piecemeal reform to efforts at social reconstruction, do we not leave the small areas of consensus that undergird specific reform efforts; do we not become stalemated by the dense controversy that envelops wider, more complex, and more pervasive change? Will potential cumulative attitudes supporting change be overcome by existing cumulative institutions supporting the status quo? If real change calls for activating and reconstructing existing institutions and processes and for mobilizing attitudes that would support such a reconstruction, is all this feasible if one encounters more and more conflicting values as one expands the reform effort?

The answer depends, of course, on the types of attitudes that are evoked as reform action moves out from the original group consensus supporting piecemeal reform to the conflicting attitudes rooted in groups and institutions affected by the broader reform effort. On the face of it one might expect that broadening the front of reform would ordinarily lead to an impasse if not a disaster. If suburban whites oppose busing, if blacks oppose segregation (or integration); if parents of parochial school children oppose more funds for public schools unless they share in those funds and if others flatly oppose aid to parochial schools; if conservatives oppose federal aid because they fear overdependence on the national government and subordination to it, how could comprehensive reform be accomplished?

The solution to this dilemma, according to many gradualists and incrementalists, is to play down the goal and to emphasize the immediate, practical job at hand. Drawing on the work of Lindblom and others, Schultze says that the "first rule of the successful political process is, 'Don't force a specification of goals or ends.'" Don't just stand there wondering what the point of the whole thing is; do something. But incrementalism has failed conspicuously to overcome the major socioeconomic problems facing the nation. To take the specific, agreed-on action often means waiting until a long-gathering problem has assumed an explosive state and everyone agrees that something must be done, even though it is too little and too late. It is to shirk the need to act early, vigorously, and comprehensively to head off a gathering crisis *before* it detonates. Small steps may simply postpone clash and controversy. The need is not to avoid conflict, even polarization, but to recognize polarization as a genuine expression of the way things are and, then, to transform conflict into a synthesis of positive change. Whether a nation can confront and overcome its toughest problems, its deepest divisions, through the process of national debate and decision depends ultimately on its capacity to define its fundamental values and to find in them guides to action.

CHAPTER **6**

Beliefs as Guides to Action

The question is whether Americans possess a set of principles or values clear and meaningful enough to enable them to define national goals, set social priorities, and systematically enact and administer policies to achieve those goals across a wide front of social and economic activity and over a long period. To take up this question is to venture into a terrain littered with snares and shrouded in fog.

For one thing, Americans are said to dislike the very idea of a national value system because it smacks of ideology, and ideology is a foreign concept, a bit sinister, the spawn of Jacobins and Bolsheviks. The ideologist is the doctrinaire, the dogmatist, the ivory-tower intellectual spinning implausible theories and plans out of a closed conspiratorial mind. Americans prefer the practical thinker, the tinkerer, the doer, the commonsensical man of action who does not let windy ideas stand in the way of getting the immediate job done.

Not only is ideology bad, we are told, but we do not have one. We are said to have no purpose, direction, value system, thought-out structure of goals and methods. Scholars have demonstrated that the mass of Americans are indeed anti-ideological, that they like the trappings and symbolism of democracy but not the substance of it, that they tend to be intolerant, rigid, and anti-civil liberties in practice. Their leaders act with more consistency, perhaps, but when the chips are down they too experiment, improvise, rationalize. The great statesmen like Lincoln and Franklin Roosevelt, even John Calhoun and Woodrow Wilson, are found to be pragmatists. All this is good, we are assured. Happy is the nation that has no ideology.

If the nation has any ideology, others tell us, it is the ideology of pragmatism. But this is not the pragmatism of American philosophers who, however eager they were to escape from transcendental absolutes and closed systems of thought, tried to see the interrelation of socially desirable ends and value-laden means. It is a bastardized pragmatism that has had the implication for principle sucked out of it and replaced by a narrowly calculated opportunism and individual self-interest. It is not an ideology; it is hardly more than a habit or instinct. To be sure, we have embraced particular ideologies such as chiliastic religions, anti-egalitarian doctrines in the antebellum South, social Darwinism, anticommunism. But these have ultimately yielded, or will yield, to the power of a truncated pragmatism.

Is it not curious, then, that most foreign observers and many American scholars find that Americans have had some kind of national credo, hazy and shapeless as it may be? Tocqueville found a powerful belief in Christianity and democracy, in liberty and (especially) egalitarianism, in majority rule—though he granted that Americans found those beliefs in themselves, in their experiences, rather than in a philosophical school. Myrdal said a century later that the central thesis of his study of the "American dilemma" was the conflict in the heart of the American between his "moral valuations" and other forces. Most American scholars exploring the web of the American belief system—Parrington, Louis Hartz, Perry Miller, Richard Hofstadter, Arthur Schlesinger, for example—have located in the American experience a wide and persistent adherence to an individualistic liberalism, though they have disagreed as to how sterile or creative that liberalism has been, or how consistent its component elements and its practical application.

Still we resist the idea. We keep proclaiming the "end of ideology," only to see new or old ideologies reasserting themselves. Few who were familiar with the philosophically arid campuses of the 1950s could have dreamed of the explosion of doctrines in the next decade. Few would have dreamed that so many politicians would soon be talking like evangelists.

This contradiction between spurning ideology as a theory and embracing it in practice arises in part from a great confusion as to what ideology is. Certainly Americans do not possess—nor are they possessed by—an ideology in the classic sense, that is, ideology as a kind of secular religion that offers an inclusive system of comprehending reality, a total theory of causation in history and society, a hierarchy of mutually consistent ends and means, a comprehensive way of life embracing moral values, social goals, and the political system, a blueprint of action. Americans do seem, however, to possess a body of doctrine that is deeply rooted in the western heritage (just as the orators say); that has been operative in American history and society; that has broadly shaped, and been shaped by, our political institutions and leaders. But this credo is inchoate and divisive, in part, because we reject ideology instead of analyzing it, demythologizing it, modernizing it, and converting it into an instrument for social progress. In Fourth of July orations and other public rituals we tend to cite as American values such all-embracing slogans as "In God We Trust," or we merely wave the flag.

Does it matter that our values are incoherently articulated? Do the people need a credo to survive and progress? Cannot they rely on day-to-day experience, hunch, calculation, resourcefulness? They can to a degree, just as an individual can. But in the long run, a nation—at least one so founded and organized as the United States—needs the sustaining and directing force of some kind of value system. This is what being one nation, one people, amounts to; without some kind of unifying bond that overrides all the divisions, the nation must slowly disintegrate or violently break up, as the United States did in the middle of the last century. Above all, such broader valuations are crucial to the process of social change. Without them people would be locked into the status quo, entrenched in local, particularist attitudes and prejudices.

Only by recognizing and reformulating the basic values dominating a nation's consciousness and the national goals legitimated by those values can political and economic institutions be seen to be inadequate and then transformed by new programs and policies. There is no logical basis, Frankel says, for moving from descriptive social theory to practical action unless value judgments are made, nor will there be a practical will to action unless such judgments are made explicit. "A social philosophy which explores the basic choices available and offers an ordered scheme of preferences for dealing with them is indispensable . . . if there is to be a translation of social theory into social action on a scale large enough to fertilize social theory and to affect the social order significantly."

LIBERTY IN EQUALITY

Our task is not to paste some ideas together and try to invent a credo, one that will excommunicate the unbelievers, but to locate, to discover, the ideas that are deep within us, to sort them out and clarify them, to analyze how they link with one another, and finally to see their relation to existing and changing institutions in American society. We can find these ideas historically in the values Americans have endorsed and rejected, in the politicians they have elected to office and barred from office, in the promises presidents have made in their inaugurals and influential congressmen have preached from their Hill, in the nature of the enemies we have fought and the nations we have allied with, in the words, such as *Liberty*, on our coins and in our national anthems, in party platforms and campaign speeches, on the walls of public monuments like the Lincoln and Jefferson memorials.

The American credo can be encapsulated in one word—freedom. Or in three—liberty and equality, or liberty *in* equality, or (in Morgenthau's term) equality in freedom. The place of these two values in the American credo must be understood in relation to each other.

Doubtless the single most animating idea in American history has been that of individual liberty. It was for life, liberty, and the pursuit of happiness that independence was declared; it was to secure the blessings of liberty that the Constitution was drawn up and adopted. But this concept of liberty was essentially negative. Governments, established churches, and other institutions had been on men's backs too long; men must be freed of these burdens to do what they wanted. These negative liberties were made explicit in the Bill of Rights of the Constitution. Men would be free of governmental restraints on free speech, free press, freedom of religion, freedom of assembly, and due process of law. The essential role of government was to remove constraints from men.

The idea of negative liberty interlocked with the most powerful economic and social doctrine of the nineteenth century, laissez-faire. Economic man must be freed of governmental impediments that might thwart him in reaching maximum efficiency and productivity. Herbert Spencer and his followers in Britain and the United States argued that the state must not intervene any more than was necessary to protect life and property; further intervention, such as factory legislation, provision for gas lighting or drainage, or compulsory vaccination, was immoral in theory as well as ineffective in fact. The less governmental power, the more individual liberty—it was as simple as that.

During the past century men slowly came to see a crucial fact— that since they lived amid a web of restraints of all kinds, personal and private, institutional and psychological, to abolish one type of restraint was to vest more control in other types; and that, specifically, the diminishment of governmental power simply gave more scope to private economic and social power, such as that wielded by capitalists and industrialists. Compared to these forces government was not a tyrant; the question was whether government could liberate men *from* these forces.

Liberty, in short, was a matter of the *reorganization* of restraints. A social or political force could be a restraint on liberty; it could also be a *generator* of liberty. No one articulated the paradox more sharply than Abraham Lincoln. "The world has never had a good definition of the word liberty," he declared in an 1864 speech, "and the American people, just now, are in want of one. We all declare for liberty; but in using the same word we do not all mean the same thing. With some the word liberty may mean for each man to do as he pleases with himself, and the product of his labor; while with others the same word may mean for some men to do as they please with other men. . . ." He used the example of the shepherd who drives the wolf from the sheep's throat, for which the sheep thanks the shepherd as his liberator, while the wolf denounces him for the same act as the destroyer of liberty. Everything turned on the social context in which a man acted. This decisive shift in the perception of the nature of liberty in a new social context was but a step toward the idea of *positive* liberty, an idea that took on increasing clarity during this century. Liberty was the capacity for effective choice among meaningful alternatives. Effective choice could be exercised by the free and full use of the institutions and procedures of society, especially of government, rather than by seeking to escape from society and government. Anyone serious about *real* liberty had to acknowledge the interdependence of different types of liberty.

Of all our national leaders it fell to Franklin Roosevelt to give the fullest public definition of positive liberty up to his time. Against Adolf Hitler's attempt to define freedom as a kind of national right to be exercised over and against other peoples, Roosevelt proclaimed the Four Freedoms—freedom from want and from fear as well as freedom of speech and religion. Then, in 1944, on the argument that "necessitous men are not free men," he announced that "We have accepted, so to speak, a second Bill of Rights under which a new basis of security and prosperity can be established for all—regardless of station, race, or creed. Among these," he said, "are: The right to a useful and remunerative job . . . to earn enough to provide adequate food and clothing and recreation . . . the right of every family to have a decent home . . . the right to adequate medical care . . . the right to adequate protection from economic fears of old age, sickness, accident, and unemployment. The right to a good education." The promises of Fair Deal, New Frontier, and Great Society politicians have in essence been extensions of these ideas.

The meaning of liberty was shifting, and so was the concept of equality in America.

EQUALITY IN LIBERTY

The Americans of 1776 made a flat moral commitment to the principle of equality except for slaves. American leaders ever since have consistently supported that commitment in their rhetoric. They have departed from it only in practice.

"All men are created equal and from that equal creation they derive rights inherent and unalienable, among which are the preservation of life and liberty and the pursuit of happiness." That was how Jefferson first drafted the famous sentence in the Declaration of Independence and it indicates the primacy of the idea of equality. (The Declaration of Rights incorporated in the French Constitution of 1791 was even more direct: "men are born and live free and equal as regards their rights.") But the words in the final American declaration were definite enough. If liberty is essential to mankind, the political philosopher Roland Pennock says, equality is essential to democracy. The famous foreigners who have inspected American democracy— Crèvecoeur, Tocqueville, Bryce, Brogan, Laski—were invariably struck by the thrust of egalitarian thought and practice in the nation's political and social life.

One reason for the power of the idea of equality in America

has been its many-sidedness and sheer ambiguity. An idea that had been equivocal in Enlightenment and even in biblical doctrine took on a variety of meanings in the heterogeneous setting of the New World. Hence the doctrine could appeal to many men with diverse interests. Hard questions emerged from the press of events. What *kind* of equality—economic, political, legal, social, psychological, or other? Guaranteed by what private or public agency, if by any? Equality for *whom*—blacks as well as whites? Equality of *condition* or of *opportunity*? This last question was perhaps the most difficult. Did equality of opportunity simply mean that everyone should have the same place at the start, and after that the devil take the hindmost? In that event, free grade school education for all might theoretically meet the total requirements for equality of opportunity. Or did it mean that there would be an attempt to equalize all the factors that during the course of a lifetime might determine the outcome? In that case, who was responsible for the equalizing?

When a general idea is limp and flexible, evolving interests reinterpret it and extract from it the specific doctrines that serve their needs. During the mid-nineteenth century King Cotton ruled an expanding slavocracy while prating about Jeffersonian egalitarianism. During the latter part of the century capitalism glorified the doctrine of equality of opportunity while managing an increasingly inegalitarian economy. By the end of it the whole nation tolerated a system of "separate but equal" in the South that made a mockery of the very equality that it seemed to celebrate. Early democratic theory in America, McCloskey said, was never systematically worked out, so that a hierarchy of ideas or ideals was never possible. This failure persisted well into the present century. By the end of the nineteenth century Americans had erected, behind the facade of egalitarian doctrine, virtually the same structure of inequality that Tawney had found in Britain. This inequality was protected by executives and legislators favoring laissez-faire; by conservative courts; by a fragmentized working class, weak trade unions, impotent radical movements.

There was, however, some erosion of inequality. Public education—America's earliest and biggest experiment in socialism—improved the life chances of millions. The right to vote had been extended to the propertyless. An embryonic labor movement had achieved some economic and even political power. Farmers were better organized. With the new century came in turn Theodore Roosevelt, muckrakers, the progressive movement, Woodrow Wilson. The Square Deal effort to pit federal power against giant corporations, and the New Freedom program to protect the little man against special privilege, gave some underpinnings to the doctrine of equality, though not to the extent the labels suggested. States passed legislation that to some degree righted the old imbalance between business and workers and farmers. The doctrine of equality was taken out of its rural context—in which it had meant essentially an equality among property owners—and applied to an increasingly industrialized society. Yet blacks remained almost completely cut off from these egalitarian tendencies; they were mired in the caste system.

Now a major transformation began to take place in the meaning of equality. The concept of equality of opportunity had originally been used as a conservative device; it meant simply that a man enjoyed equality if he was given his place at the starting line, no matter how disadvantaged he otherwise might be. "When one starts poor," Lincoln had said, "as most do in the race of life, free society is such that he knows he can better his condition; he knows that there is no fixed condition of labor for his whole life. . . ." But this evaded the whole question of how to reform a "fixed system" that operated against a worker—or a Negro—and how to create a system giving him *real* equality of opportunity. Such a system of real equality would embrace not only education but health, housing, connections, capital—all the factors that reinforce motivation and self-confidence and capacity.

No one posed this requirement better than Herbert Hoover, the apostle of individualism. While America built its society on the attainments of the individual, he wrote in the 1920s, "we shall safeguard to every individual an equality of opportunity to take

that position in the community to which his intelligence, character, ability, and ambition entitle him; that we shall keep the social
solution free from frozen strata of classes; that we shall stimulate
effort of each individual to achievement. . . ." Later, in his first
campaign for the presidency, he returned to the idea of a fair
race: "We, through free and universal education, provide the
training of the runners; we give to them an equal start; we provide in the government the umpire of fairness in the race. . . ."

Did conservatives realize the radical implications of this doctrine? If the government was really serious about equality of opportunity, if it actually wanted the individual to achieve that
position for which his *basic potentialities* of intelligence and
character fitted him, then government must be more than an
umpire; it must do much more than supply free education; *it must
intervene at every point where existing structures of inequality
bar a person from the opportunity of realizing all the potential that
is in him.* If government really did not want a person caught in
frozen strata of classes it must attack the class system itself. If
the government really wanted to "stimulate" the effort of each
individual, government must intervene early enough in a person's
life to ensure that he had a chance to enjoy or develop that degree
of motivation, self-assurance, literacy, good health, decent clothes,
speech habits, high-quality education at all levels, job opportunity,
and the other attributes that enable him to compete on a genuinely effective basis.

The nation never confronted this dilemma of egalitarian doctrine as starkly as it is presented here; Americans do not change
by amending their ideology but by amending their behavior.
What happened in effect after the catharsis of the Depression
and the fresh perspective of the New Deal was the establishment
of governmental programs that not only aimed at recovery but
guaranteed wider distribution of opportunity. Such was the effect
of social security, social welfare, protection of the right to organize, a variety of aids to farmers, business regulation, fair employment legislation, full employment efforts, health and housing

programs, as well as stepped up educational programs such as vocational training, Head Start, and the like. Even Republicans like Dwight Eisenhower were soon quoting Lincoln's revolutionary doctrine—though neither they nor Lincoln probably saw it as such—that the "legitimate object of Government is to do for a community of people whatever they need to have done but cannot do at all or cannot do so well for themselves in their separate and individual capacities." Given the structure of inequality into which people were born, given their absolute incapacity as individuals to change the conditions holding them in a class or caste system, the implications in this statement for further egalitarian efforts by government were almost boundless. Equality of *opportunity,* originally a conservative inegalitarian concept, had become in effect equality of *condition,* a potentially very radical idea.

A significant advance of this theory of equality of condition emerges from the changing concepts embodied in the writing of those who were the chief theoreticians of the War on Poverty. The original impetus expressed in the Kennedy era most eloquently in the early work of Richard Cloward and Lloyd Ohlin was based on opening the doors of opportunity, through which those excluded from the benefits of an affluent society must be allowed to enter. Juxtaposed to this was the theory of powerlessness of the poor, particularly of the black ghetto poor, developed by Kenneth B. Clark and associates in the HARYOU study, which argued that equality of opportunity was a charade unless equality of *condition* were provided, that inequality of condition made it impossible to seize opportunity offered. The poverty programs that followed were living manifestations of these theories. The language of the legislation called for maximum feasible participation of the poor in decisions affecting their lives and the promises of the Kennedy and Johnson administrations echoed this extension of the theory of equality. But most of the programs were, in effect, classic *opportunity* programs and based on the social-work model; those seeking to implement the language of the promises encountered the opposition of established power groups, especially in the northern cities, and in almost every case the national government retreated to the previous status quo (a possible exception is the continuing, though constantly challenged, support for antipoverty legal assistance programs). But the concept of equality of condition had been further extended all the same, despite incapacity to fulfill it, and the expectations of the poor had been correspondingly raised. After such increase of expectation, there can be no turning back.

THE ARC OF FREEDOM

"Democracy," said Maury Maverick, "is liberty plus groceries." Behind that artless but key simplification lay decades of groping thought and tortuous action. It had taken a long time to overcome the old and damaging concept of liberty and equality as hopeless opposites. Americans, without being wholly conscious of it, had brought about a convergence between values of equality and liberty—that is, between subvalues of liberty, positive as well as negative, and subvalues of equality, of equality of condition as well as of opportunity. No longer could we say flatly, the more government, the less liberty. But neither could we say the opposite. Everything depended on the impact of government and other restraining and liberating forces on men's actual liberty and equality. A restriction of some persons' liberties—for example, to keep blacks away from certain lunch counters—would mean a major expansion of other persons' liberties—to frequent the lunch counter of their choice (and to feel liberated in doing so). Restraint on an employer's right to block union organization of his employees would produce a considerable expansion of the employees' economic, social, and political liberties.

If these values of liberty and equality interlock at certain points, they also are in a state of tension at other points. And at some points they do not relate at all. Thus certain negative liberties, such as the right of privacy, freedom of religious thought, or freedom of conscience, are in a special category of their own. The right to hold any or no religious belief, for example, is as nearly absolute a right as one can have. But as a person moves from these almost absolute negative liberties to more positive liberties, and toward rights subsumed under egalitarianism, he begins to actualize liberties that touch those of other people. No one else is affected if a person in the quiet of his home holds attitudes of hatred or contempt toward others, or if he worships strange idols over his fireplace. A person is also protected when he stands on a soapbox and calls for laws supporting segregation or discrimination, or if he urges people to new forms of worship. But now his rights may begin to impinge on those of others—for example, if he calls on people to lynch a Negro in the crowd. His capacity to express his views and act on them, moreover, may be limited to what Dahl has called "equality of resources." For example, the right of a person to express unpopular views may be diminished by his restricted access to the mass media. Thus the more active a person's exercise of his more positive rights to liberty and equality, the more those rights strengthen or weaken associated rights of that person and of other persons.

At certain points, then, the range of subvalues of liberty and of equality coexist in various states of interstimulation and tension. Similarly, certain subvalues of equality can be carried past the range of the subvalues of liberty so that the former contradict the latter. A shift from equality of opportunity to equality of condition would immensely broaden men's capacity to maximize their positive liberties, but if a government promotes equality of condition as a single, overriding value it may "level down" the whole population to similar conditions of existence, to the point where some would no longer enjoy such liberties as intellectual and artistic self-expression, or even the right of privacy and freedom of conscience. Orwell's *1984* dramatized this possibility; it is not wholly fictitious. Artists and intellectuals who labor indefinitely in fields or factories in the People's Republic of China, for example, are less free, thereby, to fulfill their own potential, although the condition of the millions has improved.

Because the subvalues of liberty and equality exist in a state of both interstimulation and tension, we can discern a rough ordering of values that make up a kind of hierarchy, or at least a set of priorities. Because these values make differing claims on government, because they order expectations and relations among people in different ways, because they produce various degrees of cooperation and conflict among people, because they usually offer the possibility of considered decision and choice, they provide the substance of a meaningful and operational credo.

This credo is not, of course, limited to the values of liberty and equality. Other values may be significant at certain times and under various conditions. The ideal of fraternity—the third of the great trinity of the French Revolution—has gained impetus in recent years from the civil rights movement and from students and others preaching and practicing communitarianism. "Brother" and "sister" are the only titles accepted in the black community today. But the philosophical basis of this ideal is essentially that of equality as broadly defined; the two nicely complement each other. Brothers are peers. Another value, which won a good deal of attention a generation ago, is that of individuality, defined as the expression of a person's "real," autonomous self and of his capacity to attain psychic security in group situations without surrendering his power to make effective choices for himself or to maximize his self-expression and creativity. It is popularized today as "doing one's own thing." But this value too is essentially a subvalue of liberty and equality. The supreme values of liberty and equality, defined in all their scope, complexity, and texture, embrace a range of specific, operational subvalues that comprise the arc of freedom in America today.

VALUES AS GUIDES TO ACTION

Obviously Americans possess—and are possessed by—provincial and particularistic ideas—a host of relatively narrow ethnic, religious, sectional, sexual, racial, parochial, and folkish attitudes. These views, forming the structure of attitudes that dominate everyday life, do indeed in many cases thwart efforts at comprehensive reform. But in a mobile, dynamic, and increasingly cosmopolitan society, Myrdal contends, one can appeal from the narrower, tradition-bound values in men to the more general, higher, and "moral" valuations. People tend to possess hierarchies of values. The existence and extent of these hierarchies vary enormously from person to person, and any kind of rational organization of values is especially lacking among the less educated. But to the extent that Americans hold wider valuations as well as narrower ones, the former can be evoked and brought into play in the political process. There is a good deal of day-to-day opportunism as people respond to particular local situations and to local groups with attitudes adjusted to the requirements of those situations. But there is also a subtle and recurring pressure toward consistency in one's own valuations, Myrdal says. A kind of balance develops in a person between particularist and provincial day-to-day valuational attitudes and the more generalized, persistent ones. Myrdal concedes that there "*is* a great deal of practically mechanistic causation in human life, almost completely divorced from valuations. People do strive to keep their valuation conflicts under control. They want to keep them off their minds, and they are trained to overlook them. Conventions, stereotypes, and convenient blind spots in knowledge about social reality do succeed in preserving a relative peace in people's conscience." Most people, moreover, are busy and distracted with their routine life and don't worry about such matters. But modern people "*do* have conflicting valuations," he adds, "and the spread of knowledge and the increase of interrelations *are* more and more exposing them."

In their private lives people work out rough hierarchies of values—values of privacy, order, planning, spontaneity, control, permissiveness, work, play, and the like. Various of these norms come into conflict as choices must be made. David Lilienthal notes in his diary: "A phrase that sticks in my craw: it is only out of *conflict* that we know what 'values' we believe in. We ourselves don't know about 'values' except as we are forced to make *choices of values* and that comes, usually, through a *conflict between values*, forcing such a choice. A tough doctrine, perhaps, but right: the fact that it is tough means that it is right *for the young.*"

In the public sphere, too, people make choices and in doing so help establish a collective hierarchy of values. It is the task of government to reflect, legitimate, and act on this hierarchy. Thus the Supreme Court defends the absolute value of freedom of religious belief by voiding a provision of the Maryland constitution requiring a declaration of belief in the existence of God as a prerequisite to the holding of public office. Certain kinds of free speech are protected; other kinds are not, including the famous action of calling "Fire" in a crowded theater. Rights of conscientious objection slowly change as popular and unpopular wars are fought.

Perhaps the best example of American government responding to a hierarchy of values is the "preferred position" doctrine. This doctrine was the official view of the Supreme Court during the 1940s and is still supported by a number of justices. It expresses the view that First Amendment freedoms hold the highest priority in the hierarchy of constitutional principles and that courts thus have a special responsibility to question laws that may jeopardize these freedoms. Any law that, on its face, limits First Amendment freedoms is presumed to be unconstitutional. The justification of this doctrine is that the country could experiment with social and economic change without much danger because mistakes could be remedied through the political process, but that tampering with free speech was perilous because it might close off the very political channels through which error could be remedied.

Of countless other examples that could be cited of the capacity of government to discriminate with some precision between preferred values and secondary but key values, one must suffice. Soon after its establishment, the National Labor Relations Board had to judge between the rights of workers to organize unions of their own choosing without undue interference by employers, and the right of the employer, like that of any other citizen, to express his views publicly as to whether his or any other employees should organize. The Board ruled that the "higher" right of the employer's freedom of speech must be protected, but in such a way that improper economic power would not be directed against the workers.

Full agreement on such matters cannot always be reached, of course. Since unanimity over the scale of values and the hierarchy of ends is impossible and undesirable, as Lucien Mehl has said, there will always be disputes, conflicts, and tensions in society. This is good, for resolving such conflict and dispute is the food and drink of democracy. The question in any event is not agreement on blueprints of ends and means but whether we can find in our values reliable guides to action.

To do so calls for a reversal in our usual "pragmatic" way of thinking. As practical men, we typically decide on an action that will "work" in terms of some early concrete satisfaction for a specific person or group; if we bother to justify the action beyond immediate satisfaction we do so on the basis of some convenient value that we can locate after rummaging around in our grab bag of principles, often ignoring other values that might be more important. Principled realism demands that we draw our lines of action directly and firmly from our most cherished values, as the Supreme Court, for example, has been doing from the values of liberty and equality in recent years. We then, to the degree possible, reorganize our means to fit our ends rather than the reverse. If, for example, our system of federalism—which is glorified as virtually an end in itself but which is actually only a mechanism of government—is found in fact to stand in the way of realizing such ends as liberty and equality, the principled realist seeks to modify the means before he truncates the ends.

Of course, we never work on a tabula rasa, and often the institutional means will be so immovable or unchangeable, as in the case of foreign policymakers dealing with one hundred or so separate national sovereignties, that the means must severely limit the ends. Further, to move back from ultimate ends to means-laden ends and ends-laden means is to encounter a continuum of such enormous complexity that only students of causation could begin to understand the interplay of "individuals, interests, institutions, and ideas"; our theories of causation are too primitive to be of much help here. We must keep in mind, moreover, that in a pluralistic context there are combinations of instrumental means and ends, implicit or explicit means, and "proximate end-interests," as Von Vorys has usefully called them, as well as single means that can be used for different ends—all of which make for enormous complexities for the theorist, let alone the man of action. But these complexities, however important, must not obscure the central point—ends must, as far as possible, shape means.

We can conclude that the wider valuations of Americans do reflect their collective and strong libertarian and egalitarian instincts, that these valuations can be laid out in an array of rough but guiding priorities. I believe that the fundamental values of freedom are to be found to a much more marked degree of intensity in the people as a whole than in their separate groupings in states, communities, and interest groups, and that this has been demonstrated repeatedly in this century in the reelection or retention of the Roosevelts, Wilsons, Trumans, and Johnsons on the one hand, and, on the other, the repeated defeats of egalitarian and libertarian proposals (such as public housing) on the local level, especially in state, county, and city referenda. The issue is not the existence of a vast potential of generosity, compassion, tolerance, and willingness to share with others; the issue is whether that potential can be mobilized politically and converted into a movement able to win power necessary to translate values into programs. The issue is whether our government can be transformed into an instrument able to carry out such a program. The issue is whether we have—or can develop—leadership capable of both perceiving and pursuing the means that are necessary to carry out such great ends.

Part III

❀

THE TASKS OF UNCOMMON SENSE

CHAPTER 7

The Transformation of Government

I am contending that:

1. We face the 1970s—and the bicentennial of 1976—with a failing political system and with an overload of explosive potentials for disruption and deadlock.

2. Neither working through the present political system nor overturning it through revolution can solve these problems.

3. As "realists," we have measured action by the test of practicality, of "what works," ignoring broader, longer-run consequences. These habits of thought have made for a derangement in the relation of our ends and means.

4. The extent to which we can make means serve ends depends on the context of action. In foreign policy, the circumstances are generally beyond our power to control and hence we must beware of set doctrine. In domestic policy, we have a far greater opportunity to shape means to serve ends.

5. Common sense having failed to overcome deep-rooted poverty and environmental blight, we must and can locate in our overriding national principles clear guidelines for a collective attack on these conditions and for the defense of individual liberty.

6. Since poverty and blight are each rooted in clusters of

mutually supporting forces that defy short-run efforts and single "solutions," only an intensive, comprehensive, persisting, and concerted effort will overcome the underlying causes of the problems.

7. The vital tasks now are to transform our governmental system into an instrument that can convert, on a planned and systematic basis, the economic, social, and political forces now sustaining poverty and blight into forces that alleviate these conditions; to generate strong and steady political power to support such governmental efforts; and to mobilize talented and purposeful leadership at every level of our political system. How to achieve these tasks is the subject of these concluding chapters.

THE FRAGMENTATION OF GOVERNMENT

The revolutionary ends of 1776 were, on balance, egalitarian and democratic; the constitutional means of 1787 were, on balance, antimajoritarian and elitist. This is an oversimplification, but a useful one. "Conservative in philosophy and method, revolutionary in purpose—such has been our political tradition from the beginning of colonization," Hans Morgenthau has summed it up. This conflict has been at the heart of our political system, never more so than today.

The men of 1776 threw off the yoke of a "foreign" government so that the popular aspirations of Americans could be realized. The men of 1787 struggled to channel and control those aspirations toward the goal of an orderly, stable, and balanced polity. Government was a necessary evil and had to be cribbed and confined. "Free government is founded on jealousy," Jefferson said, "and not in confidence. . . . In questions of power, then, let no more be heard of confidence in man, but bind him down from mischief by the chains of the Constitution." What had happened to the great faith in the people? "A dependence on the people is, no doubt, the primary control on the government," Madison said, "but experience has taught mankind the necessity of auxiliary precautions." So, in effect, the Framers divided power between the national government and the state governments, and in turn distributed national powers among two houses of Congress, the president, and the judiciary.

The Framers planned brilliantly. They did so because, as theorists as well as practical men, they knew how to ensure a clash of interests among government officials by linking the latter's personal interests to a diversity of contending sections, ideas, and economic groups. They realized that it would be useless to put power into the hands of different men if those men combined and conspired against the people's liberties. They would keep the leaders in conflict by making it their interest to be in conflict. "The great security against a gradual concentration of the several powers in the same department," wrote Madison in his penultimate argument in Federalist 51, "consists in giving to those who administer each department the necessary constitutional means and personal motives to resist encroachments on the others." And in case anyone did not know what he meant by personal motives, Madison added: "Ambition must be made to counteract ambition."

The result has been a vast dispersion of power throughout the American political system, the fragmentation of collective efforts to realize the egalitarian ideals of the Declaration. This dispersion remains most obvious in the original distribution of powers between the national and state governments, and within the national government. But the dominant purpose of the Framers—to provide government with adequate power (for their time) but to morselize and tame it—in conjunction with the geography, makeup, and habits of the American people, serves to fragmentize further almost every portion of the sprawling political system, and the related systems of education, business, labor, and other foci of the social dynamic.

Thus within Congress today we find not only the original bicameralism, which gives each chamber an absolute veto over the other. Within each house power is further dispersed into the congressional and presidential parties, into a host of policymaking committees, into subcommittees and factions of those committees, into the hands of chairmen and ranking members of the committees, into a whole separate taxing and appropriating system that is itself widely diffused. The Rules Committee in the House, which can block or cripple key measures, and the power of a small group of senators to kill bills through the filibuster, are cunning little embellishments of a system designed by subsequent, mainly anonymous "framers" in the last century to thwart majority rule through government.

The dispersion reaches all through the system. The executive branch is, in many respects, simply a holding company for departments, bureaus, and a profusion of offices, agencies, corporations, authorities, bureaus, and more. Many of these become little fiefdoms that join hands with a committee or subcommittee of Congress, and at the same time act as a well-organized interest group to form a delta of power as rigid as one of Buckminster Fuller's triangles in resisting pressure from outside, especially pressure from the president. The federal judiciary still holds a veto over certain types of legislation passed by Congress and approved by the president—a veto that has escaped criticism by liberals in recent years because the court has been issuing decrees with egalitarian and libertarian impact. Finally, the dispersion of power within the states, and particularly the crazy quilt of local boards, taxing districts, commissions, special authorities, public corporations, piled on top of already fragmentized city and county governments, is a grotesque caricature of the whole system.

How then does anything get done? How does government govern, at least from day to day and in this area and that? Because Americans have proved adept at knitting together in practice what the Framers separated in principle. Operating in their separate spheres and enclaves, responding to different and often conflicting constituencies, the political and economic brokers variously cooperate, compete, and collide with one another in endless negotiations, compromises, arbitrations, improvisations, trade-offs, standoffs, threats (to pull out of the negotiations of the coalition, to trade elsewhere, to ally with some other group, to strike, to organize a new group or party), and sometimes carrying out those threats. It is a horse trader's paradise, a lawyer's heaven.

What if leaders or groups so fundamentally disagreed that bargaining and compromise became impossible? Such a turn of affairs—a polarization between real radicals and true-blue reactionaries, for example—would tear the system apart. But this has rarely happened in America because the brokers have been fundamentally agreed on their ends and their means. Their ends have been something called liberty, especially negative liberty, and some kind of rough equality, especially equality of opportunity in the nineteenth century sense—plus the institutions in which these values are embodied. (Another example of ends and means swallowing each other.) But these ends or values are still so ill defined, so diffused and generalized, that they serve mainly as ad hoc, year-to-year bases of compromise rather than as clear guides to collective action. A poignant example of how a cloudy set of values can permit compromise was the late nineteenth century separate-but-equal formula that kept blacks and whites segregated while purporting to grant equality to the Negro. Only a principle that meant different things to different men in practice could have permitted such a formula to persist for so many decades.

The great defense of our system of brokerage is its immense resilience. For one thing it has survived—survived world wars, civil war, depressions, mass migration, urbanization, and all the rest. Too, it has encouraged an enormous amount of resourcefulness, invention, imaginativeness, experimentation. It has permitted a great deal of incremental progress in certain sectors. It has made for an open polity, an accessible government, a good deal of individual initiative, great looseness at the joints.

But this system has also exacted a fearful price. It has thwarted collective efforts to realize systematically and soon enough the goals implicit in our revolutionary tradition. It has tended to deal with symptoms and dramatic manifestations rather than with rooted, structured social evils and illnesses. It favors the groups—the more affluent, knowledgeable groups—represented by the abler brokers. It discriminates cruelly against the unorganized or ill-represented masses of people. It is always too late; hence social malaise breeds and proliferates for years before action is taken. And the system makes for crisis, which serves only as a temporary catharsis; conditions fester until there is a dramatic breakdown, national attention rivets on the crisis—Watts or Kent State or Attica—a solution becomes, for a time, the first priority for all concerned; actions are piecemeal, with little attention to long-term needs or effects; the crisis seems to be resolved; the brokers turn back to business as usual—and the underlying ills persist.

One other price of the system has been intellectual. Power in the political system is so diffused that any official or group or institution wielding a modicum of influence—a corporation, the president, organized labor, the Pentagon, Mayor Daley, even university officials—looks formidable in comparison. And so a vast literature has sprung up about the naked power of such entities —of the military or the munitions-makers or the CIA or a variety of others, or combinations thereof, such as the military-industrial complex or C. Wright Mills' "power elite" of military, big business, and government. These persons or institutions *do* have undue power, but only relatively because the governmental system is so weak. The unhappy result is an attempt by radicals to diminish the power of leaders and entities they oppose rather than to build up the powers of the only political institutions that can act for collective needs—a national political movement and the national government.

THE CONSERVATISM OF GOVERNMENT

If all the veto groups that thrive in a fragmented government had the same veto power, the system might at least seem equitable, however impotent and archaic. But, in fact, the vetoes are unfairly apportioned. In Congress, for example, the Rules Committee, which was once a means of expediting majority rule in the House of Representatives, has become the agent of the conservative Republican and Democratic congressional parties in the lower chamber. The filibuster in the Senate, which would appear to be a neutral device available to any outraged minority, has had its most important—some would say only important—effect in stalling, weakening, and defeating civil rights measures. The seniority system vests extraordinary power in the hands of older men from safer districts, a combination that guarantees a bias toward negativism and conservatism.

The only political mechanism that is unduly biased *against* conservatism is the Electoral College. Its winner-take-all arrangement, combined with politicians' impressions (or superstitions) that organized religious, ethnic, racial, and labor groups swing big industrial states to liberal presidential candidates, has biased the presidential electoral system toward a liberal presidency. This is the bias that Senator John F. Kennedy brilliantly fought to retain in 1956 when opponents of the winner-take-all rule proposed to substitute a plan for proportional or fractional representation. The winner-take-all rule survived, but as a lone bit of favoritism toward liberalism. The strongest vetoes lie in the hands of conservative groups.

What if liberals were able to achieve their loftiest dreams of congressional reform—abolishing the filibuster, the seniority system, noncompetitive districts, the power of the Rules Committee? Would this remove the conservative bias from the present fragmented system? Would it make the system equally responsive to moderate-conservative and liberal-radical forces in this country? Unhappily no. No system—not even a system without vetoes—is neutral.

To disperse power is to place it in the hands of numberless minority groups. The more organized the groups, the stronger they typically will be. People are not equally organized into interest groups. The more affluent have more memberships in interest groups just as they have more of the other desired things in life. The poor man who may belong, at most, to a local church group or PTA cannot compete with the affluent farmer, industrialist, skilled worker, or professional man who pays dues to, is active in, and is represented by, a union, a professional organization, a taxpayers' association, various civic groups, or any of a host of other organizations. And neither can compete with the financier who is on the boards of a bank, a foundation, a church, and a university. Not only in group memberships but in everyday contacts—getting around, attending meetings, following events in the newspaper, writing the editor, avoiding jail, giving money to a party or candidate—the rich man wields more influence than the poor man.

The problem goes deeper. Even if it were possible somehow to equalize group memberships across classes and statuses, a fundamental bias against egalitarian government would remain. As we have seen, dispersed political attitudes and behaviors do not necessarily reflect the national "pooling" of attitudes and behaviors. In politics the sum of the parts does not necessarily equal the whole. The generous, egalitarian, sharing attitudes of national majorities may not be found in the localities, at least in such force and persistence. There is an irrational tendency toward parochialism, inwardness, self-protectiveness, suspicion of outsiders. There is, also, a rational tendency not to act generously when generosity hurts, when one has the feeling that someone is taking advantage of his generosity—when other states or communities, for example, keep taxes and welfare standards low in order to entice industry from the more benevolent areas. There is a practical failure of empathy.

To fragmentize is to conservatize. Revolutionary leaders have always seen this; that is why they have insisted on mass solidarity and collective action. The moral is no less important to those who wish to conduct a revolution within the system. Aside from a few social experiments in certain innovative states, the great egalitarian movements in this country have been national in participation, doctrine, and impact. It has been the national leaders mobilizing followers from all sections and classes of the people who have been mainly responsible for social progress.

It all seems to defy common sense. The best government would seem to be the most local government, the most tangible and visible government, the most accessible government. But it has not worked out that way. Fragmented, impoverished local government with its withered tax base and often amateurish officials is, on the average, the most inadequate and invisible, and often even the most inaccessible, government. Decentralization of ghetto communities often leaves them simply more vulnerable to economic, social, and political forces beyond their control. Most important, decentralized government is not the kind of means that can come to grips with and resolve nationally produced problems. Only the national government can.

THE NATIONALIZATION OF GOVERNMENT

But the national government does not. We are witnessing, as Theodore Lowi contends, a crisis of public authority—power without values, without purpose, without standards, without discrimination or finesse. The whole structure of authority, rationale of power, above all the capacity of *united states* to deal in a unified way with social evils—all these have come into question during the 1960s and confront us even more sharply in the present decade.

Our first task is to establish the effective authority of the national government over all significant conditions and forces that relate to the three national priorities—the defense of civil liberties and civil rights, the abolition of poverty, and the protection of the environment. Authority means dependable, systematic, and uniform control everywhere in the land, not just in the South or the North, the cities or the suburbs or the country. It means, for example, control not only of social security but of job training and school lunches, not only of highways and public works but of economic development, not only of the results of human migration and industry relocation but of the migration and the relocation itself. It means not only the "federalization"—actually the nationalization—of welfare but of health, employment, housing, education, and of environmental protection and development to the extent that these activities impinge significantly on the three priorities. It means vesting in the national government the capacity to set standards nationally, to plan comprehensively, to finance adequately, to coordinate closely, to follow through persistently. It means the re-creation of the national government.

It means first of all the strengthening of the presidency. This is something neither conservatives nor most liberals will want to do—conservatives because of their traditional suspicion of national executive power, liberals because presidential foreign policymaking in recent years, especially in Vietnam, has given them a frightening glimpse of "arbitrary rule." But the presidency must be the prime governmental agency of social progress, not because it is an ideal institution but because there is no alternative to it.

First, the president must have the power to plan and the will to do so. Planning mechanisms have steadily grown in the White House ever since Franklin Roosevelt established the short-lived National Resources Planning Board. The executive office has burgeoned with domestic and foreign policy councils, program analysts, budgeteers with planning responsibilities, legislative clearance agencies, and a recent planning-programming-budgeting system, all of which had planning responsibilities or implications. One of the chief antiplanners in the White House has been the president himself, Democrat or Republican. As politician in chief in a fragmented system, he feels he can remain on top by not planning too far ahead, not making commitments, not setting a course that can be thrown off direction by congressional and other opponents. He seeks to conserve what limited power resources he feels he has. No one needs more to be educated in planning than the president himself—and no one so directly and dramatically experiences the failure of planning.

The issue of planning is shot through with other ironies. Until quite recently, as John Fischer has pointed out, "the American credo held that planning was just dandy for businessmen but was forbidden to politicians and civil servants. *Public* planning was regarded as a sin, indulged in by godless Communists but unthinkable for any right-minded American." In recent years it seems to have become acceptable for the federal government to plan in sectors or pieces, as witness the Tennessee Valley Authority, the national highway system, the space program, but general planning still seems to frighten presidents and people. President Nixon may have given a boost to the idea by strengthening the planning machinery of the old Budget Bureau, in his new Office of Management and Budget. The executive planning machinery, however, is still primitive.

The president must have far greater fiscal authority than he has today. On this score there has been some progress in recent years. The Employment Act of 1946 provided a legal mandate for fiscal activism, as Sundquist points out, and the creation of the Council of Economic Advisers in the White House and of the Joint Economic Committee in Congress established strong advisory groups at both ends of Pennsylvania Avenue. But advice should not be equated with power. Twice President Kennedy requested standby authority to reduce taxes on a temporary basis, and President Johnson urged Congress to alter its procedures to permit rapid action on temporary tax reductions if recession threatened. Both presidents were rebuffed on Capitol Hill.

Congress can be expected to cling jealously to its basic fiscal power. But the president should have the power, within broad limits set by Congress, to alter the timing and application of tax laws. He should also possess ampler latitude on spending. Over the anguished outcries of congressmen he exercises today the power not to spend in categories for which Congress has appropriated. There is little that congressmen can do about presidential inaction except, quite properly, to appeal to the public. The president should also have more authority to transfer unobligated balances of any funds already authorized by Congress. All this is for the sake of giving the president flexible, versatile fiscal resources to enable him to invigorate, direct, and control closely the immense administrative effort necessary for the attaining of priorities.

The main object of reform must continue to be Congress. If an analyst were ever able to uncover the prime *institutional* reason for the lagging social progress of the 1950s and the upheavals of the 1960s, surely it would be the structure of negativism built into both houses. The destruction of civil rights measures on Capitol Hill is a grievous example. After a half century of repeated efforts at reform it has become simply banal to urge the obvious—the abolition of the filibuster, the seniority system, and the other procedures that have turned Congress, in the area of broad social progress and political reformation, into one of the most negative political institutions in the western world. That Congress should enter the last third of the twentieth century, an era of tumultuous change in almost every aspect of human activity, with these archaic arrangements intact is nothing short of grotesque.

But here again the abolition of evils is not enough. As the proponents of the seniority system insist, Congress must have leadership, and who will do the job if the committee chairmen do not? The obvious alternative is the elected leadership of Congress—the speaker of the house, the majority leaders and whips and policy committees in both chambers. It has been repeatedly demonstrated, however, that the party leaders cannot mobilize support in Congress for the big, controversial, divisive bills (except in crisis) without far more party backing and party discipline than they have been able to evoke. This is why it is imperative, as indicated in the next chapter, that the presidentially led party be well enough organized and directed in the states and congressional districts to be able to sustain the party rank and file in Congress in standing behind the leadership on the big bills.

Only if Congress is nationalized in this way can it ever resume the positive legislative role that the Framers anticipated. A fragmented Congress—especially one artificially skewed to the right—could never assert its authority except through obstruction of the president and the people, and this negative role is bound to be increasingly unpopular in an age when great tasks must be performed. At best, however, strengthening the party foundations of Congress may take time. What can be done in the meantime?

The immediate solution is to accept the implications of the fact that for a long time the presidency has been the "architect of policy" and Congress has wielded the veto power. This major shift in constitutional roles can be extended, at least on a short-run basis. Congress could grant the president sweeping, blanket policymaking powers within broad limits in domestic areas that demand priority action. The president's policies would stand unless vetoed within a set period by either simple majorities in both houses or by a two-thirds or by a constitutional majority in either. This is not a new idea; Congress has accepted this kind of procedure in dealing with presidential reorganization plans and in a number of other fields. As a safeguard against "presidential tyranny" the basic grant of power to the president could be given for a limited period such as two years, and could be extended or suspended after that.

Congress would retain other important powers. It could be responsible for passing a national commitments resolution that would stake out the basic domestic priorities for the succeeding two or four years. It would keep both the legislative initiative and veto in a host of policymaking areas outside the priorities sectors. It would serve as the central arena for debate over programs and policies. It would investigate, expose, spotlight, evaluate failures to carry out these commitments. It would serve as the national ombudsman. Individual members of Congress, as

Ralph Nader has suggested, could act on citizens' complaints, especially consumer complaints; gain significant information from corporations and trade associations through "public letters of inquiry"; serve as litigators, "moving from one branch of government to another to spur enforcement of laws or development of fairer procedures in the regulatory and service agencies . . . "; and work on congressional reform. This last item alone could demand a good deal of congressional thinking and energy. As a minimum Congress needs to have sufficient power so that, if the presidency became unresponsive to national need, the legislative branch could act as a balance wheel, and a prod to action, as the courts have done to compensate for executive and legislative failures in protection and extension of civil liberties and civil rights.

Ultimately the bureaucracy will be the testing ground of the government's capacity to realize priority goals. No part of our system—not even local government—has appeared to sink so swiftly in popular esteem as has the executive branch in recent years. Not only do the young radicals view it as darkly as did the old-time apostles of laissez-faire. The nadir must have been reached in 1968 when the Democratic party, after having elected most of the twentieth century chief executives who presided over the burgeoning of the bureaucracy, charged in its national platform that the "massive operations" of the executive branch "contributes to and often results in duplication, administrative confusion, and delay." Pommeling the bureaucracy, even by the hand of its friends, is an ancient and perhaps somewhat salutary sport. But the executive branch is too important to be left to the old jokes and bromides. How can it be converted into an instrument for ending poverty and protecting the environment?

One step has already been proposed by Mr. Nixon—the regrouping of dozens of federal agencies into a smaller number of larger, more coherent, more functional departments. It is a pity that the president found it necessary to claim too much for the idea in offering it to Congress. It is by no means revolutionary, but a small step in bringing together related functions and ending some of the existing scatteration. Even the Nixon plan does not solve the problem of related functions that cut across the proposed new departments—for example, environmental problems that link up with both "human" and "economic" affairs.

Reshuffling will make little difference unless the president can establish firm control of the new structure. Franklin Roosevelt demonstrated how a president sometimes can keep more control of a divided administration than of a highly structured one. As Roy Ash, the main author of the Nixon reorganization plan, has granted, "The eclectic structure of today's departments and agencies, whose missions are often overlapping, places the President's office alone at the pivot point on many detailed or individual issues." At the pivot point—that is precisely where the president's office must always be, and of course one man's detail is another man's crucial link. Regrouping of functions may help the president carry out his program, but not if he merely exchanges a host of little baronies for a few big ones.

Thus serious efforts to tighten presidential direction and responsibility must go much farther than reshuffling. The line of command between White House and action agencies in the field must be drawn taut no matter what the nature of the intermediate grouping or structure. This means that the "delta of power"—the mutual protection society of agency, congressional subcommittee, and beneficiary interests—must be dissolved. Agencies like the Federal Bureau of Investigation and the Army Corps of Engineers, which have simply been more visible in their resistance to presidential and even departmental control than many other agencies, must be brought back under the authority of the only man in the executive branch who is elected by the people. The overall policymaking of those curious relics of a bygone age, the "independent" regulatory commissions, must be restored to popular control. Corporations, authorities, and the other autonomous hybrids must give up their independence from presidential, and hence public, direction.

All this is needed, all this is orthodox, and all this is inadequate. If the president and his administration are to achieve their priority missions, a much more flexible, versatile, and action-oriented instrument is needed.

The *administrative task force*, an old concept in the military and an embryonic one in civilian administration, has potential as such a national instrument. A task force is a more or less temporary grouping of different arms or services to accomplish a specific purpose. The White House has long brought officials over from the agencies to work with presidential aides on specific problems. The institutional and psychological home of these aides usually continues to be their agency, to which they have long-run commitments. What has been done on a short-term, day-to-day, ad hoc basis with recommendations, however urgent, "writ in sand," as a former cabinet member described them, should be organized on a more systematic, mission-oriented, visible, and even dramatic basis. Task forces should be established in the executive office but with responsibility for implementation held by skillful professionals for continuous direction of priorities operations. The agency officials, who now tend to be delegates to the White House from their departments or bureaus, should be converted into agents of the president, *agents able and willing to generate support, direction, unity, and innovation in their various agencies behind the president's priorities*, though always evaluated and measured by Congress.

What the nation needs is not some kind of top permanent civil service along British lines. That elite body succeeds in Britain because it operates within a unified administrative system. What is needed, in the top-priority areas, is a cadre of talented, vigorous, mission-oriented "presidential agents" whose formal position and paymaster will be far less important than its political and psychological relation to the president and the national sense of purpose. This cadre must be sufficiently based in its departments or bureaus to know their administrative possibilities and limitations, to locate their abler men, to grasp their relations with other agencies sharing functions—in short to discern and to help mobilize their potential resources. They must work with, or detour around, cabinet members, department heads, and bureau chiefs as the objectives require. But they must be sufficiently part of the White House establishment to remain truly agents of the president.

But tightening its direction of the national executive branch is only part of the job for the achievement of urgent national priorities. The president must assume full responsibility, in the priority areas, for the functions and effectiveness of the whole governmental system.

THE LOCALIZATION OF GOVERNMENT

Nothing has challenged the political ingenuity and common sense of the American people more than the effects of the division of powers between the national and state and local governments. Presented with constitutional fragmentation, the people have found endless ways of joining hands to deal with common problems across the divides left by the Framers. Well over a century ago Tocqueville wrote that he had never been more struck by the "good sense and practical intelligence" of the American people than in the manner in which they eluded the numberless difficulties resulting from their Federal Constitution. The federal grant in aid to states and lower bodies, with federal strings attached, is but one of the devices used to meet the need for collaboration while maintaining the symbols of separation.

The latest expedient is tax sharing. It is proposed that the federal government simply hand out the money, with no strings at all. The idea seems the acme of common sense. If the states and cities need more money and cannot raise it, and if they are weary of president and Congress telling them what to do, and if Washington has that marvelous resource called the graduated income tax and other fiscal resources, why should not the people in their states and localities get "their own" money back?

The trouble with most of these practical arrangements and hopes is that they have not solved basic problems or showed much promise of doing so. They have usually helped meet immediate, specific needs, but one can say of state and local governments as a whole what Lowi said of the cities—they are well run but badly governed. They make the street lights work and do a hundred other tasks—sometimes remarkably well, but often remarkably badly, witness sanitation in the urban ghettos—but they do not and cannot deal with the rooted problems that are the concern of this book. Revenue sharing, for example, is no revolution but an abdication, as Max Frankel pointed out. "The President, Congress and their bureaucracies were never meant to be merely tax collectors," he wrote. "They were meant to govern, to attain a wider reach and a broader view of the national interest than any local regime, and indeed they have until now progressively done so. They were meant to preside over a system of multiple tax collection and spending that allows money to pass up the ladder of governments for services best managed by a higher authority and to be redistributed down the chain for services best administered at the state, city, county, village, or school-district level." The central flaw in Mr. Nixon's scheme, Frankel stressed, was that it would ignore this system in the name of reforming it.

Tax sharing would not begin to solve the main problem of state and local government—its fragmentation. The dismal picture has often been painted—the states with their factional legislatures, inadequately staffed governors, mediocre civil services, and scanty revenue; the multiheaded county administrations; the 80,000 cities, school districts, townships, water control districts, pollution control districts, all piled one on top of the other in a jumble of conflicting powers and splintered authority. This too is nothing new; it is over thirty years since Harold Laski looked at American federalism and labeled it as negative, slow, destructive of necessary standards of uniformity, as dangerously dependent on compacts and compromises, and as tending to leave "the backward areas a restraint, at once parasitic and poisonous, on those which seek to move forward"—in short, as obsolete.

The great divide now separates city and suburb even more than city and country. Here, again, New York City is the striking example. Its suburbs contain about nine million people, who make up in themselves the largest "city" in the nation. Most of the inhabitants have not only broken their occupational and social ties with the central city; they have declared a kind of cold war on it. Through zoning and other devices they seek to stem the flow of the outward migration of poor people, especially blacks, into their preserves. But even if suburbanites wanted to help the inner city, as some do, they would be powerless. Suburbs are so Balkanized the inhabitants can hardly govern themselves. The four counties closest to New York contain 548 governmental units, including municipal, town, and village governments and a multitude of school, hospital, cemetery, sewage, and other districts. All are administratively and fiscally autonomous; almost all have taxing power, limited though it is. These counties lie in New York State, ruled by a governor and legislators who feel neither fiscally capable of dealing with the central city nor politically motivated to do so. Other parts of the city of "New York Suburbia" lie in Connecticut or New Jersey and thus comprise a whole extra set of Balkan enclaves.

The system is so badly conceived to solve national problems that its excess of failure has produced an excess of utopian solutions. It has been suggested that the states be abolished, that counties be wiped out, that a city such as New York either become the fifty-first state or secede, that new regional governments take over the functions of state governments, or that federalism simply be abolished, leaving presumably, one big central government. Many of these schemes are not only nonsense, they are dangerous nonsense, for they would divide the energies of reform and attempt to separate what is inseparable. Let it be said flatly: the American people will not accept, at least in the foreseeable future, any major tampering with the structure of American government. Like it or not, suffer from it or not, they want the forms of federalism kept intact, whatever happens to its content, just as the English wanted the monarchy retained whatever happened to its powers. Americans might accept major governmental changes in time of crisis, but a constitutional amendment takes months to pass, and it is virtually inconceivable that interest in such an amendment would be sustained enough and broad enough to push it through both houses of Congress by two-thirds votes and through the legislatures of three-fourths of the states.

What could be done, then, to realize basic changes in the operations of government without challenging the essential form of government?

We must be prepared to innovate boldly, not by tinkering but by an overarching mobilization of money, talent, and energies. I propose that the task force concept be extended down into the states and localities. The federal government would establish "presidential" agencies in several hundred regions throughout the country. These agencies would work directly under the supervision of the president and his executive office, bypassing departmental and bureau levels if necessary. Their jobs would be to integrate all governmental policies, federal, state, and local, that relate to the priority areas. In the program to eradicate poverty, for example, they would administer—or supervise the administration of—those aspects of welfare, employment, job training, education, industry and manpower relocation, health, housing, urban renewal, school lunches, child nurseries, literacy programs, local transportation, and other activities or programs that related to poverty. For environmental goals the regional agencies would administer—or supervise the administration of—those aspects of public works, land use, economic development, antipollution programs, highways, recreation, preservation of open land, forest policy, solid waste disposal, suburban development, conservation, protection of wilderness areas that were necessary to fulfill the presidential commitment. Unlike the present regional Federal Executive Councils, these agencies would have *power*.

The size of the regions or localities would vary widely. They would not necessarily follow present state or municipal boundaries. They would not, indeed, follow any logic except that of realizing priority goals; here, as always, ends must rule and guide means. Some regions would be the size of New York City or even of the whole New York metropolitan area; some the size of a county; some the size of a large watershed; some the size of a particular rural, urban, or suburban complex. The larger regions would be subdistricted, where existing institutions, economic and social patterns, and other factors permitted, into local regions of perhaps 100,000 to half a million people. The new regional agencies would not ordinarily replace existing public or private agencies except for certain regional offices of the federal government, which would be brought into the larger operation.

The regional federal agencies would be headed by one person, not by a council or committee or board. That man or woman would be responsible to the president of the United States. He would be armed with the powers of the president as clearly and specifically delegated to him and as relevant to his responsibilities in his region. His job, rather than advising and overseeing and prodding, would be to unify and if necessary direct all federal, state, and local agencies—from HEW or HUD offices to county welfare offices to community action programs or poverty councils —in carrying out the priority programs. His great powers would be legal and financial—legal in that he would be clothed with the constitutional power of the federal government, financial in that he would have the resources of the federal government in spending and in granting or denying funds to state and local agencies and to private and quasi-private groups. He would do on a local, planned, systematic basis what for years the federal government has been doing on a national, uncoordinated, improvised, and only half effective basis—bribe, prod, inspire, and otherwise induce the state and local agencies to do what they should do and sometimes want to do.

Since this kind of proposal is bound to conjure up images of regional gauleiters or local czars, certain aspects must be clarified.

The state and local agencies would continue to exist in their present form with most of their present functions—all the functions, at least, that did not directly relate to the priority programs. Community action programs designed to involve the poor in participation in policies affecting their lives would be strengthened, not weakened, and protected against inroads of those jealous of this new distribution of power. Local agencies and programs would, moreover, in many cases help to administer the priority programs, but only under the close supervision of the regional federal agency. The test would not be the holding of formal authority but the achievement of goals. The administration would be regional and local because the federal and other officials would be operating "close to the people." But the standards and goals would be national because the priority programs can be realized only on a national basis.

Purposeful social change is essentially a matter of the planned application of power. The vital task of all the agencies, public and private, would be to bring the instruments of social change and human improvement jointly to bear on the institutions and persons concerned. They would act on the central lesson we have learned from our failures of recent decades—that purposeful social change can be effected only if the processes of change operate directly and jointly and symbiotically on specific human conditions. Thus the task of the federal agency would be, through leadership, management, persuasion, cajolery, financial inducements, and legal authority, to mass all the local agencies behind clearly defined goals. Nothing less than this will do if we are really serious about our "unconditional war" on poverty or our national commitment to protect and enhance the environment.

Today we talk about goals and standards but it is loose talk, for we do not empower our institutions to realize our high aims. We do not confront or combat the dispersion of power that creates endless veto centers to which opponents of our goals can appeal. What happens now is that when an administrator tries to carry out priority goals he eventually encounters governmental or private resisters who can appeal to constituencies that lie beyond the administrator's power to reach. The obstacle could be a congressman appealing to a bloc or committee of Congress; a corporation depending on its influence with a local municipality (an influence magnified by the corporation's ability to flee the area, or to threaten to do so); a construction union that turns to its national office; a federal agency that appeals to its "mother" bureau in Washington, which in turn appeals to a constellation of congressional, bureaucratic, and private interests; a metropolitan special-function authority that calls upon the congeries of local governments that established it. These rights of appeal must, of course, be protected in a pluralistic, constitutional system, but what we need is national power that will not crumble before the veto centers but rather will either associate the dispersed power groups with its priority goals—which are in effect the priority goals of all the people, not simply a favored few— or will reach these goals without vested-interest support.

What about local government, popular participation, open decisionmaking, and the other devices that have been developed and glorified in recent years? Here again the test must be the realization of goals. The main purpose of a poverty council presumably is to attack poverty. If, in the process of doing so, the council also develops a good deal of grass-roots participation, especially by the poor themselves, all well and good. That participation also is a goal. But it is not the main goal. Better to abolish poverty without much participation than to have a great deal of participation and not do much about poverty.

Here as always we must put first things first. Means, no matter how beneficial, should not be substituted for ends; they should only be applied to ends. Any effective official must understand that to do his job he must involve local leaders, rank and file elements, and their institutions. Men of the quality needed for the regional federal officials would understand that. As in many other instances, means and ends are interrelated. The abolition of powerlessness of the poor is a necessary correlate of the abolition of poverty. To play a part in one's own destiny is to be taken more seriously by those in power, and those who are taken seriously are enabled to move from poverty. The problem arises when the mechanisms, however democratic and participatory, are substituted for actual social reform—that is, for changes in the lives of people who are supposed to be the beneficiaries of the priority programs. Too often those in power who are not serious about change provide the appearance of power to the deprived as a substitute for actual change.

We must understand, in short, the crucial distinction between advisory and participatory groups *in* government and such groups *as* government. Not only can the latter not govern—that is, cannot produce necessary change—they are also exceedingly vulnerable to being preempted by the forces they are supposed to regulate or master. We are only too familiar with antipollution boards composed of pollutors, draft boards composed of middle-class, middle-aged men, local public utility boards unwilling and unable to investigate the industry, and hosts of advisory councils themselves most in need of advice. Ironically, the actual influence of many of these participatory and advisory councils within the present fragmented system has been much exaggerated. They would probably have more influence at least on matters relevant to priority goals if they operated under the direction of regional federal agencies—that is, if they directly advised men who actually wielded power—and if they were taken seriously by the wielders of power as ombudsmen, as boards of review and accountability.

One cardinal advantage of the *localization* of federal power—which is what we are talking about here—could be enormous flexibility. In appearance, the establishment of a host of federal agencies with comprehensive and centralized power might seem to suggest rigidity and regimentation, if not monolithic government. In fact, these agencies must be strong enough to adapt themselves to the infinite variety of local geography, people, resources, governments, and other institutions; lean and flexible enough to respond to need. In one region the role might be mainly supervisory, as existing agencies might be adequate to realize priority goals. In other regions the existing institutions might be so weak that the federal agency would have to create a whole new infrastructure of decision and administration. Most areas would fall between these extremes. The nature of the regional conditions would vary enormously, as in the case of a rural area losing population or of an urban area overwhelmed by it. The key guideline would be the attaining of national goals through an infinite number of "mixes" of local leaders, institutions, and mechanisms.

The task forces themselves need not become a permanent fixture of government, at least in any one sector; their role would be for the middle run, pulling existing government agencies together, setting standards for them, energizing them. Properly directed, and quickly deployed from one part of the governmental system to another as priorities demanded, they could be a continuing source of stimulation and renovation of major bureaucracies, which otherwise tend toward ossification. They could do so at the state and local level too. In the long run, the states and localities must take up their full share of the burden of government, including priority goals. As Benjamin Baker has suggested, most of the reforms proposed in this book for the national level are equally necessary at the state and local. Governors and local executives should have adequate staffs and fiscal and legal power. They should have the support of strengthened local and state parties. Their power to lead should be bolstered by providing them with talented administrative lieutenants, by widening channels of recruitment, and by increasing the executive's control over environmental and social planning.

To some a proposal to federalize and localize priority programs will seem a radical step. Yet it seems to be an idea that has been struggling to be born. Regional government has been quietly growing up around us in recent years. Over 140 councils of government—voluntary organizations of municipalities and cities—

have been set up across the country to tackle areawide problems. Most have been established under the incentive of federal grants. These councils generally have only powers delegated by member governments and hence they are weak; they have done more planning than acting. But the embryo is there. And when Mayor Lindsay calls for the creation of "national cities" he is acting in the spirit of this trend; but if the main problems we confront are national in cause and scope, why be content with federal cities? *Every* city, rural area, and suburb should make its contribution to national action, and should be its beneficiary.

Do these proposals overplay the capacity of government to solve problems? Only if we conceive that government—an institution made up of human beings and comprising the biggest and strongest team available to us—must always be the fragmented, fumbling institution we are familiar with. Only if we have given up on government as beyond hope of transformation.

In the proposed regional agencies and in the presidential task forces that would direct and empower them, the central aim would be to harness resources and to assign priorities in line with the national commitments to a hierarchy of purposes. Government would be, as it is at its best, not an autonomous bureaucratic entity but an instrument to draw together funds, talent, public and private resources, for intensive assignment to the primary commitments. Just as the federal government was able in World War II to rally scientists, engineers, foundations, business, industry and labor, public and private agencies, material and human resources without limit to mount the offensive; just as the government combined its own powers and tapped the strengths of other institutions to build nuclear weapons and to plan and carry out the space program, so government must now compel and persuade the investment of national energies to solve the urgent human problems of this century. All this demands much of government; it demands more of the people, acting through their political institutions.

CHAPTER 8

A Party Fit to Govern

The birth boom of the late 1940s will produce a voting boom all through the 1970s. Twenty-five million voters will be eligible to vote for the first time in 1972, including ten million eighteen-to-twenty-one-year-olds, Frederick Dutton estimates; another sixteen million will become eligible by 1976 and eighteen million more by 1980. The over-thirty-fives will still cast about two-thirds of the total vote during most of the decade, but the sixty million new young eligibles will produce a powerful and, perhaps, volatile element in the political chemistry of the decade.

At the start of the decade many of these young eligibles were immensely disaffected from the existing political system. Only sixteen percent of students, according to one study, felt that the major parties offered any alternative. Many young people hesitated to register to vote or sought out dissident party groups or announced that they would vote not the party *or* the man but the issues. Some talked about forming or joining a fourth party; others turned their backs on the whole electoral and party system and drifted toward a variety of alternatives ranging from guerrilla war to privatism.

Clearly there was a profound unrest in the political system. Was a new political tide rising? What direction might it take?

THE COMING PARTY UPHEAVAL

Along with the enormous expansion of young eligible voters one can discern a number of factors that could transform the whole context of politics in the 1970s:

1. The two major parties are showing unusual signs of disarray and decomposition. American parties have never been models of leadership and organization, especially at the national level. But more than ever there seems to be erosion at the foundations. Local and state party organizations, if they have survived at all, exist as highly personalized, patronage organizations which, once the party's candidate has been nominated, recede into the background as the candidates take over. The exceptions, such as Mayor Daley's organization in Chicago, are so few as to excite wonder.

The Democratic party is especially feeble and vulnerable. It has a paper army of tens of millions, but these troops fade away at the critical moment. The National Democracy, in spite of a marked superiority in party registration and party self-identification over the Republicans, has won three out of six presidential contests since World War II. Over the past decade it has allowed the GOP to hold the governorships of New York, California, Illinois, Massachusetts, Michigan, and a host of other key states in areas that were once bastions of the party. Democratic majorities persist in Congress, but this too is a paper affair; the national party has no control over—indeed, has little relation with—most of the Democratic leadership in the House and Senate.

2. Voters seem increasingly restless, unsettled, variable. They have been splitting tickets to an almost unprecedented degree. Burnham and others have found a recent and rather steep increase in independents—an increase that has roughly approximated the decline in persons strongly identifying with one of the major parties, especially the Democratic. Analysts used to dismiss independents as generally uninformed, uninvolved, unaware. But a second kind of independent is coming to the fore—the voter who knows only too much about the performance of the parties and

candidates and shifts back and forth from election to election
and from party to party as he seeks to realize his political values.

3. One of the most reliable signs of portending changes in
major party politics—the rise of third parties—has been con-
fronting us for several years. Third-party movements do not
always forecast party transformation; but since Jefferson's time
there has been no basic party change without preliminary froth-
ings and crosscurrents manifested through third-party activity.
The power of the George Wallace movement—Wallace won a
larger percentage of the votes than any third-party effort of the
past century save for Theodore Roosevelt in 1912 and La Follette
in 1924—indicates that large numbers of voters cannot find a
place in the present two-party system.

Not only are Wallace's "little people" rebellious, adrift, and
available to the highest bidder, but millions of other Americans
both on the left and on the right are disenchanted by the old
politics and are casting about for new political vehicles. A year
before the 1972 campaign, a liberal-radical coalition was planning a fourth-party ticket that hoped to gain power by the end
of the decade on the ground that neither major party was able
to bring about change. John Gardner's Common Cause and a
variety of other nonparty, nonpartisan organizations have gained
from boredom and frustration with the old two-party politics.
Many of these organizations are ill adapted to participation in
two-party electoral politics. Doubtless they will form one more
volatile factor in an unstable political compound—until they
ultimately make a commitment to a party.

4. The black migration into the cities—one of the biggest and
most portentous migrations in history—continues; the white migration to the suburbs accelerates. Negro voters form a political
mass heavily Democratic in most cities and able to elect mayors
and councilmen but divided, disorganized, and caught in an
infinity of frustrations, suddenly aware that political power does
not bring with it, necessarily, economic or other institutional
power. The suburbanites in their school, housing, and zoning laws
steadily erect barricades against black encroachment. Left in the

South are millions of blacks long ago cast off by the Republicans, not yet organized or mobilized by the Democrats, many segregated and devitalized politically in their rural ghettos.

One city symbolizes the passing of the old political ways. New York City Democrats split in all directions over a mayoralty candidate and end up with a nominee who is a standing contradiction of the liberal, urban, innovative thrust of the New Deal party. A city with a minuscule Republican party elects a Republican mayor, who is later repudiated by the Republicans. A Conservative party, a Liberal party, and various specialized ethnic and economic-interest parties turn the electoral arena of New York City into a frenzied game of King of the Rock. The mayor then becomes a Democrat. Two-party politics in other cities show similar signs of decomposition. The Democratic mayor of the second largest city, Los Angeles, is temperamentally and programmatically closer to Barry Goldwater or George Wallace than to Hubert Humphrey or Edmund Muskie. For decades most cities have found it difficult to adjust their internal party politics to the nation's politics. A two-party balance nationally tends to throw the major parties into imbalance locally, with the result that competitive politics was transferred from a battle between parties to fratricidal conflict within parties. But, in recent years, the problem of the parties in the cities has been not merely imbalance but decay.

Behind these disintegrative political forces are economic and technological ones. The remarkable combination of rising prices and rising unemployment led not only to disillusion with the Nixon administration but doubt that either party could provide both full employment and price stability. The class system continues to change; the old traditional division between an upper, middle, lower middle, and working class, with all their subclasses and with a separate black caste, seems to be evolving into far more complicated forms that cannot be easily embraced by a two-party system. Under the impact of postwar technology the old class-occupational pattern, as David Apter sees it, has been evolving into a new pattern of the technologically competent, the technologically obsolescent, and the technologically super-fluous. The new professional-managerial-technical elite tends to be more politically cosmopolitan and government-oriented than the socioeconomic elites of the last century. If it cannot fit into the "bourgeois" heritage of the Republican party, it has almost equal difficulties with the Democratic.

Add to these technological forces the political impact of the electronic mass media, which give the great public a direct confrontation with leaders and issues without intervention by the parties, and to which the volatile younger voters have been intensely exposed; add further the violent impact of Vietnam, which deranged the Democratic party in 1968 and could lash back at the Republicans any time during the next few years; add to these acts of violence and accident; and one has a sense of the tumult lying ahead. Historically this kind of upheaval has often been the prelude to fundamental change.

THE PATTERN OF PARTY CHANGE

Looking back on almost two centuries of American political development, historians have found five critical periods when the nation underwent fundamental political transformation. The elections during these periods were more than the usual sparring over which party would win an election, gain brief control of patronage, and exert limited influence on policy. These elections signified a major change in political alignments, a long-term alteration in the nature of the people running the government, and important changes in government policy. They left their stamp on the entire ensuing generation of political activity.

The first of these great transformations occurred around the beginning of the last century, when Thomas Jefferson and James Madison organized a political movement for liberty and equality that broke the Federalist hold on the Congress and the presidency. The Jeffersonian Republicans dominated the next generation of the new nation's politics. In the 1820s another egalitarian movement, receiving much of its impetus from western farmers as well as eastern workers, began to renovate the aging Republican "establishment," build a new structure of party politics, democratize the presidency, and transform the whole style of American politics. The Jacksonians struggled mightily with the Whigs, eventually overcame them, and left their brand on the 1830s and 1840s. The next critical election period, from the mid-1850s through the Civil War, saw the death of the Whigs, the conquest of the Democratic party by the Cotton Democrats of the South, the rise of a new Republican party with a strong antislavery cast, the disruption of the old party balance, the election of Lincoln, and civil war. The new Republican party acted for a coalition of business, labor, farmers, Civil War veterans, and Negroes that dominated American politics for three decades after Appomattox. Populist upheaval, farm unrest, labor ferment, and the depression of the early nineties brought a challenge to this Republican ascendance—a challenge that produced a conservative counterrevolution with McKinley and a new political alignment reflecting the power of organized business and its credo of individualism and "equality of opportunity." Coming to office thirty years later in the midst of the Depression, Franklin Roosevelt fashioned a new coalition of Al Smith Democrats, union labor, disaffected farmers, and the South—a coalition that, save for the addition of Negro support and the slow desertion of the South, was ascendant for another thirty years.

Looking back, we see a certain logic and neatness in these great political movements. They usually required at least several years to achieve momentum and win election victories; they invariably projected a popular new president into power; they usually lasted twenty to thirty years, and in dying they helped produce a new transformation. In fact, the movements were untidy in doctrine and amorphous in membership; they collected hosts of opportunists; and both leaders and followers were unclear as to ends and means. Many third parties and assorted smaller, collateral movements muddied the political waters, with mixed long-run effects. Many movements failed to achieve their original aims.

As Christopher Lasch has noted, the People's party finally disintegrated into the Farm Bureau Federation and allied farm lobbies, radical labor into craft guilds, feminists into pressure groups, socialists into romantic anarchists, blacks into cooptation and compromise.

Only the most prophetic could have discerned which of the early gropings and stirrings would strike sparks among masses of people, kindle a growing flame of discontent and protest, produce massive organization, and overthrow the existing regime. But one quality was characteristic of (though not limited to) all the successful movements and hinted of their future impact on government. All movements in their own ways preached equality and liberty. Even the counterrevolution of the 1890s advertised a doctrine of libertarianism that could, given the misty contours of American ideology, be closely linked with the great teachings of Jefferson.

It is now thirty-five years since Roosevelt finished patching together the coalition that would give him three more presidential election victories, Harry Truman reelection in 1948, and John F. Kennedy a narrow victory in 1960. The "Roosevelt coalition" may be finished or it may be giving way to a new Republican ascendance of the type that Kevin Phillips has described. Or perhaps it is being transformed into a new Democratic coalition. Or is something else happening that may bring the whole era of party battles, as we have known them, to a close? And must we be mere witnesses, or at best passive participants, in one more "inevitable" cycle in American party history—or can we actually help determine the content and direction of the coming flood tide in American politics?

THE CONCEPT OF A MOVEMENT

The existing party system might be able to contain the restless, brooding forces of the contemporary scene for some time. The absorptive power of a rubbery, loose-jointed enterprise is enormous. The two major parties have the virtues of their defects; they may be archaic in national organization and primitive in machinery, but they are as hard to kill as the medieval serpent; when one head is cut off at least one more may grow. The party system has survived profound changes in American life—industrialization, world wars, labor and farm unrest, civil war, depression, violence. It has outlived all those who prophesied its demise.

But things are different today. The leaders of the national Democratic party—that is, the likely presidential candidates of 1972 and 1976—have committed themselves to libertarian and egalitarian values to a degree hitherto unmatched even in the party of Jefferson, Jackson, and Roosevelt. The political requirements of 1972 and 1976 will tie them even more tightly to these goals.

Thus we have the ominous prospect of presidential candidates promising liberty and equality while the parties they seek to use as vehicles become more impotent than ever to carry out those promises. Ever loftier ends, ever more limited means to those ends—this is a recipe for such a dislocation between popular demand and institutional capacity as to portend disillusion, disruption, and breakdown in the nation's politics.

That breakdown might come slowly; more likely some spark— a climactic struggle in the cities, a case of student or black slaughter surpassing even Kent State or Jackson, a sudden onslaught by Hanoi in Vietnam leading to retaliatory escalation by Washington—will set off an explosion strong enough to disrupt the existing political equilibrium and unloose a flood of new political energies. What form might these energies take?

One possibility is the disintegration of the two-party system into its four component parts. Each major party is divided into two parties in Congress, these parties, in turn, resting on a cluster of supporting forces. In the past the presidential and congressional subparties in each party have managed to combine forces in order to win the presidency, only to relapse into their old rivalry as soon as policymaking got under way again. In 1972 the struggle over fundamental values may be so intense that the four parties could find compromise impossible and hence might enter the presidential lists as separate entities. The situation may be reminiscent of the 1850s, a decade which, as Burnham has pointed out, was preceded by both significant declines in participation and by a growing fluidity of voting support for the old parties. The bursting apart of the old party system into four parties in 1860 was the prelude to civil war.

Another possibility is even more depressing, but less likely. A combination of black-white confrontation, continuing inflation and recession, student violence, and a bad turn of events abroad could simply cut through the foundations of the existing parties and reduce organized political life to a congeries of protest movements, radical action groups, third parties, and remnants of the existing two parties clinging to their states and enclaves. This could be the setting for the emergence of a modern man on horseback.

Of course, the old system might continue to work. The Democrats, for example, might stay together through 1972 and 1976, once again nominate a slightly-left-of-Democratic-party-center candidate such as Stevenson, John Kennedy, Humphrey, or Muskie, offer the usual liberal platform and promises, and seek to govern through the existing political and governmental machinery. Could such conventional politics succeed in the 1970s? The Democrats barely brought off this kind of old-time operation in 1968, and, in any event, failed to win the election. The Democratic convention in Chicago that year exemplified the process of disintegration in the party. Some Democrats were nominating a candidate, some were protesting in the streets, some were fighting the protestors, some were putting into nomination a black man for the first time in history, some were pushing through the most liberal platform in the long life of the party. The Democrats were doing almost everything except act as one *party*.

All these possibilities suggest that we must live through the 1970s under a political gun with a hair trigger. Any real pressure will produce an explosion that will tumble political walls in unpredictable ways. An unpleasant prospect—but common sense would tell us that there is not much we can do about it. In complex, intractable situations the prudent course is to take one step at a time, plan only a short way ahead, hang on to the old guidelines, and hope for the best. In short, to muddle through. But this is the kind of course we have been following in our political and economic life in recent years, with marked lack of success.

It might be uncommon sense to ask whether we could plan a course of action that would (1) act directly and consistently on the basis of our fundamental values of liberty and equality; (2) hope eventually to seize control of political events rather than responding to them; (3) enable us not only to win an election but to win a government. We have noted the epochal turning points of American politics over the past two centuries. Is it possible to *create* a critical election, to *make* a period of planned political change? Or must such great events come only as a result of accident, the concatenation of events, the separate and incoherent decisions of millions of men?

Let us begin with the concept not of maintaining a political party but of invigorating a national *movement*. By movement I mean a broad-based, issue-oriented set of popular impulses that cut across existing party and group lines, and a wide array of leaders at every level of American society, all holding values rooted in the American heritage of liberty and equality. The vehicles for the two most event-making periods of American history in the last century were not political parties but political movements. Jefferson and Madison organized a popular undertaking that was only dimly aware of the nature of a party. The antislavery, pro-labor thrust of the 1850s embraced far more than the embryonic Republican party. These movements ended up building parties but their original impetus came directly from popular protest and affirmation and from issue-conscious leadership.

A movement, unlike the party as we know it, is first of all value and issue oriented. It exists not simply to win the next election or to place its leaders in office but to win power in such a fashion and on such terms that it can *govern*—that is, it can convert values into goals, goals into policies, policies into social change and progress.

Does all this sound theoretical? It is. But listen to a most practical politician, a Democratic candidate for United States senator, after being beaten in part because his party turned out to be an inadequate foundation for a successful campaign.

"The whole basis has changed," John J. Gilligan told a reporter. "The whole undergirding of the old coalition is gone—cultural, social, ethnic, economic, it's all gone." He was convinced that the Democratic party had closed out the Roosevelt era, when its power grew from a number of groups all united and seeking their own economic self-interest. The party must now put together a new coalition that he called the "constituency of the concerned." Instead of leading, the Democratic party had found itself with the old power brokers, now conservatives instead of liberals, still maneuvering for advantage within the old coalition, "taking adversary positions, gouging, butting. . . . They are not evil men. They are just irrelevant."

Gilligan talked about the "20 per cent" who knew that the system was arrayed against them. "The real question today is will there be enough activists attracted to politics, not out of protecting what we've got but out of altruistic motives of extending our benefits to others, who can join with that 20 per cent and form a new coalition of the concerned."

That was in 1968. Gilligan won the governorship of Ohio in 1970. The Democrats carried key elections throughout the country. Perhaps with success the idea of a coalition of the concerned began to seem less urgent. But Gilligan's warning hung in the political air.

STRATEGY FOR A COALITION

By starting afresh with the idea of working through a new, nationwide, citizen-politics movement to defend our liberties, end poverty, and safeguard the environment, Americans could build a "coalition of the concerned" around these goals. This movement would be based on principle rather than expediency; that is, it would mobilize popular support on the basis of advancing programs and enacting policies rather than merely electing people to office. Europeans are more familiar than Americans with this kind of movement, but in this country it need not be weighted down by the ideological burdens that have impeded so many egalitarian parties on the continent.

Five groups could make up the core of such a coalition. First, the poor, especially the urban poor, who would serve as the foundation as well as the chief beneficiary of radical coalition politics. Second, the blacks, already a key voting bloc in many city and some state elections. Third, that enormous pool of the young. Fourth, organized labor, the biggest, most economically powerful, most politically mobilized group of all. Fifth, sizable sections of the white collar, middle class sectors.

Could such a coalition coalesce? In recent years some on the left or right have been triumphantly seizing on the tension among these somewhat disparate elements. Union labor and the Negroes in particular are said to be increasingly unwilling to live together politically. But the significance of this split has been much exaggerated. About two and a half million trade unionists are black. Several million white unionists are so integrated with blacks in shop, core city, or even urban suburb that the community of interest is quite close. To be sure, millions of other union members in construction and craft jobs, some of them hard hats, are hostile to blacks; some local strikes have had racial overtones; some Negroes become union leaders and take on the prejudices of their white peers; and other upwardly mobile blacks—teachers, professional people, technicians, and the like—manage to flee the ghetto by migrating physically to the suburbs or psychologically to middle class status. But the great majority of blue collar unionists will continue to support liberal-labor-left politics; and even more will do so given leadership that can dramatize the imperatives of unity and the common stake in government action. After all, with all its failings, organized labor over the last several decades has regularly taken the lead in civil rights, democratic planning, economic and social reform, and egalitarian measures in general. Any effort at social reform without the participation of the bulk of organized labor cannot be effective.

Even a coalition of labor, the poor, the blacks, and the young would not be broadly based enough to win control of the presidency and both houses of Congress. Support from middle class voters would be imperative. This is a class usually dismissed by radicals as hopelessly bourgeois, capitalist-minded, and anti-labor. But the old shopkeeper image is all but archaic. Today substantial numbers of middle class people are on the front lines of the technological revolution in education, space, science, government, urban problems, medical services. Many of them are union members. Most are relatively well educated.

The key to the middle class mind may be more psychological than economic or social. It might seem logical that middle class people join with conservative elites to protect their jobs, status, and incomes against working class egalitarianism and black aspirations. Many of them do. But many of them, nurtured in family and school on the American credo of liberty and equality, are intellectually or psychologically prepared to acknowledge the grievances of lower income Americans and to work with them. This is not to say that the middle class is, or ever will become, a solid bastion of social progress. It will always be divided. But it should not be written off, as C. Wright Mills sought to do by labelling it available to the highest bidder. Not only has the middle class, however reluctantly, given its children to form the cadres of left-wing battalions; the parents are the great suppliers of manpower for local charities, Red Cross, PTAs, and other community organizations that, in their own way, are devoted to the American creed. Many can and will make a commitment to social responsibility on the national level as well.

So much for the core elements of the coalition. What political strategy might such a coalition pursue?

The movement might reject party politics altogether. It might act as a super-pressure group, publicize its doctrine, work on government executives, legislatures, and bureaucracies from the outside, support or oppose candidates offered by the existing parties. This is often a good strategy for minority interest groups seeking to maximize their power in the face of competing interests. But it is not a good strategy for a majoritarian movement seeking effective control of government to realize overriding national values. It would reduce a great cause to one more organized minority competing for ad hoc power in the day-to-day shuffle of interests. Exercising public power means dominating men in office. By acting outside the party system, by simply helping elect or defeat nominees selected by existing parties, the movement would cut itself off from the direct exercise of power.

The movement might form a new party—a third, fourth, or fifth party. This is an enticing strategy for those tired of the old party politics and eager to challenge and perhaps replace either or both of the existing major parties. One could start from scratch, write an uncompromisingly progressive platform, point toward the capture of national power without being diverted into an endless series of state and local battles, enlist millions of persons turned off by the stale, compromising, opportunistic politics of the existing system. It would be a heady experience but the difficulties are all but insuperable.

It is not only that no third party in a century has beaten both major parties at the polls; history is always waiting to be made. It is not simply the enormous organizational, legal, and financial obstacles to serious third-party efforts; one can assume that a movement with great moral impetus could overcome these. The main barrier is the attachment of millions of Americans to the Democratic party. That party may be in disarray; it may be decaying; it may be losing some activist support to the independent ranks. But all studies of the attitudes and behavior of the great body of voters demonstrate that mass support of the Democratic party is one of the most persisting, widespread, and influential factors in modern-day politics. To millions of voters, especially in the lower income ranks, the Democratic party still is the party of Al Smith, Roosevelt, and Kennedy and perhaps also of Jefferson, Jackson, Wilson, and Johnson.

The obvious strategic implication of all this for the movement is, as Michael Harrington has urged, to form a new, radical political party, but not as a third or fourth party. We must have, he said as the 1960s ended, "a new party capable of winning a democratic majority for a radical program. How do we get it? The most obvious, logical and exciting answer is to start a fourth party to challenge the Democrats, Republicans and Wallaceites. Only it won't work—or, more precisely, it will work only in the interest of Richard Nixon and the Dixiecrat-Republican coalition in Congress." Harrington is a good witness here, for as chairman of the Socialist party in the United States he would much prefer, as he admits, that the Socialist party realize its ancient dream of becoming the great mass, popular party to the left of the New Deal party. But he knows that this kind of strategy is not possible in the American circumstance.

A PARTY FIT TO GOVERN?

What must a party do—what must it be made to do—to be worthy of power and able to wield it in the 1970s?

1. It must be *goal-minded*. It must be radically libertarian and egalitarian in both the literal and symbolic sense of that adverb. In its program and leadership it must show its absolute intention to get to the roots of our national problems—which will mean mobilizing political energy along every public and private channel of social change. Symbolically it must stick to the principled but tolerant left, rejecting the easy compromises and opportunistic half measures of the past.

2. It must welcome *clash, controversy, dissent*; it must shake agreeable habits of consensus and compromise. At every level from precinct committee to national convention it must be an

arena for argument, policy debates, platform-making, minority reports. For the thousands of young people turned off by politics-as-usual it must be where the political action is. A time will come for uniting the party and massing its strength, but that unity and strength would be meaningless unless it emerged from open clash and debate.

3. It must be a *national* party. It must yield no major section, social class, interest group, or generation wholly to the opposition, because some people from every part of society will rally to a party of high purpose. Hence it must reach out to every region of the country, finding common purposes that transcend the little concerns of local fiefdoms, so that it can present itself to the disaffected millions in the country as worthy of national responsibility. Its state and local platforms must be consistent in means and ends with national goals.

4. It must be *reform*-minded, beginning with itself. It must learn how to raise party money from the millions, as radical parties in other nations have done. It must risk the processes of democracy in its councils—especially in selecting delegates for the national convention and establishing its rules.

5. It must be both *inclusive* and *exclusive*. It must welcome, proselytize, and recruit members on the basis of one test and one test only—belief in the goals of the party, as defined in the platform. The millions of blacks and young people and lower income people outside the party system are skeptical of it, but many of them are willing to listen, to be convinced, and to be involved. No party can lead the way to progress in the 1970s that does not draw in these alienated people. But the party must know how to *exclude* too—exclude those who do not support the main programmatic thrust of the party and those who would use it only for their personal, opportunistic ends.

These are harsh tests. Could either of the present major parties meet them? Years ago the Republicans were the progressive, reformist party of the nation. The GOP served as the vehicle for the most powerful and long-lasting coalition the nation has ever known, and Negroes and industrial labor were two of its main components. Some Republicans today dream of a new coalition of blacks, white businessmen, skilled labor, and ethnic groups. But time seems to have run out on the Republicans. Today they can count on only a tiny percent of Negro support at the polls. Labor switched parties during and after the Depression and generally is still solidly in the Democratic camp. Some of the Republicans' best talent, from Wayne Morse to John Lindsay, has deserted them. Their main base is in the suburbs, with all the advantages and disadvantages appertaining thereto. During the middle run, at least, they are far more likely to follow a tactic of opportunism, living off the errors of the Democrats, than to take direction either toward the principled left or the principled right.

Without drastic reform, the Republicans today could meet none of the tests of the modern party. The GOP does not have firm goals; its platforms consist mainly of grand rhetoric and a multitude of small promises. Rather than welcoming controversy, it is notorious for settling its differences behind closed doors and presenting a bland face to the public. It is not a national party because it has virtually broken off relations with the core cities and, especially, with the ghettos. And it is reform-minded only to a small degree; it has sought to broaden the range of its convention representation, but formulas that will permit minority-group representation only on the basis of actual participation in state party activities will not significantly boost the numbers of young people and blacks in Republican conclaves. Nor is reform along these several lines at all likely; many of the reformers have been leaving the party.

And the Democrats? The Democratic party is on the verge of becoming an irretrievably middle-aged party—fat, flabby, conventional, living off victories it did not wholly deserve, as in 1964, and still shaken by blows it could hardly comprehend, as in 1968.

The Democracy is usually described as a collection of state parties; it can better be pictured as an assortment of senators and representatives with highly individual and varying political views and with mainly state and local political preoccupations; plus a national chairman and staff desperately trying to remain afloat financially; plus a national committee serving as a holding company for fifty or so state organizations, which are themselves holding companies for a host of personal factions that are a cross between guerrilla battalions and Chinese war tongs; plus an occasional city organization with the power of Mayor Daley's machine; plus a few local committees that are models of organization, vitality, and concern with issues; plus—and all too often—local committees that are concerned only with jobs and political minutiae between elections and bestir themselves into torpid activity when they have a local candidate they wish to push. All this—at least at the national level—changes when a Democratic president enters office, but then the national machinery becomes simply an appendage of the White House, with no real structural alteration.

How build a national movement out of this mélange? In part through spirited leadership committed to the party's national goals. In part too by strengthening the national institutions of the party. As it is, the party assumes a national posture in convention assembled for a frenzied week once every four years, and for another two or three months when, under the proddings of the candidate and his staff, elements of the party, with much creaking at the joints, feverishly convert themselves into the semblance of a national apparatus. This apparatus dissolves once the election is over, whether its candidate is successful or not. The way to build a lasting national party apparatus, pursuing round-the-clock, round-the-year party activities, is to strengthen it in areas that are relevant to national candidates and officeholders—that is, in the nation as a whole, in the states, and in the congressional districts. This would call for a *nationally oriented* party organization in congressional districts; a *nationally oriented* party organization in the states; and a *national* organization firmly rooted in the above structure.

Of many possible avenues to such change, two can be mentioned here. The delegations to the national party convention, now elected more democratically than ever, should be given some permanent status, both at the national level and back in the states and districts. They could form the core of state and district leadership. And the national party ought to meet annually, or at least biennially, in a small, workable convention, just as most democratic parties in other countries do. A few hundred delegates elected on an equitable basis would debate party platforms and choose a party chairman, who would direct the affairs of the party and serve as its responsible national spokesman. In the fourth year the conference would give way to a regular convention to nominate a presidential candidate.

The idea of an annual party conference has been urged for years in the Democratic party, and the reaction of the national party establishment—to the extent that it has reacted—illustrates much of what is wrong with the party. It is feared that ideological elements would get out of hand, young people would demonstrate and try to take over, the party's dirty clothes would be washed in public, all the differences and cleavages in the party would emerge—and all in front of television cameramen and newspaper reporters looking for a fight. Perhaps so—and so what? Better by far to have an annual blowing off of steam than a quadrennial bloodletting. The Democratic party thrives on controversy, assuming some controls (and broad controls for debate and decision could be established and enforced). Trying to conduct its affairs in a safe and sane way, in the context of the 1970s, can only mean the decline and entrophy of the Democratic party, and a merging into the style and character of the Republican party.

The Democratic party has a fair record of reform. The Democrats abolished the two-thirds rule for presidential conventions in 1936; they outlawed the unit rule in 1968; and in between they put increasing pressure on southern Democrats to come to the conventions with mixed, integrated delegations. In the aftermath of the crisis convention of 1968 the McGovern-Harris Commission shaped guidelines controlling the choosing of delegates to the 1972 and 1976 conventions; it barred state party rules or practices preventing any Democrat from exercising full and meaningful influence in the delegate selection process. Discrimination on the basis of race, color, creed, or national origin in particular was outlawed. The McGovern-Harris Commission, the O'Hara Commission, and other national and state units have been hard at work to democratize the selection of delegates to future conventions and the operations of the convention itself. Some of the reforms may go too far, may inhibit vitally needed party leadership and encourage minority factions, proportional representation, and other arrangements that could make for anarchy if not chaos in the party process. Still, the Democratic conventions in this decade will probably be the most fairly apportioned and representative in history.

The Democratic party has long boasted of being the inclusive party; during the 1970s this boast will be put to the test. Inclusiveness could be a grand strategy for the Democrats since they cannot reestablish themselves as the majority party and the party in power unless they attract groups that could compensate for the loss of the Solid South and for the shrinkage of the old farm and rural components of the party. The party must make a persuasive approach to the progressive elements in the middle class of the new industrial society—to professional people, scientists and technicians, teachers, managers in private and public bureaucracies. These are the people Eugene McCarthy appealed to so effectively.

The party must particularly welcome liberal Republicans. As a practical matter, the Democrats need to attract every potential friend into the party because they need every bit of support they can get for the tasks ahead. As a matter of principle they need the intellectual help of liberal Republicans. Some will worry that a deep and unbridgeable gap may open between a liberal-radical and a conservative-reactionary party. Whether polarization takes place will depend mainly on the response of the Republicans to a liberalized Democratic party. But polarization is not to be feared in a country where millions of centrists and moderates control the balance of power. In a two-party system neither party will ever be ideological in the European sense. John Lindsay summed up the situation well shortly after he joined the Democratic party:

"Changing parties has been a fresh breeze in my life. . . . I feel much freer about my own beliefs and I wonder a little bit about what I was doing all those years. . . ." He said that he had been thinking about the truth of the argument that both parties had to cover a broad spectrum. "What is wrong now with a coalition of progressives, from both parties, Republicans and Democrats, who think alike instead of the tortured, twisted, underground arrangement we have now? Just because we haven't had that kind of coalition for 30 or 40 years doesn't make it wrong. I remember my own unthinking repetition of the 'broad spectrum' argument over the years."

But the Democratic party must know how to *exclude* too— and on the same basis. The time has come for bluntness: there simply is no room in the Democratic party for conservatives. This does not mean purges; in the last analysis no one, not even conservatives or opportunists, should be barred from the party or expelled from it if for some reason they wish to be part of it. The party should simply become so clearly, forthrightly the reform-minded, liberal-radical party of the day that those who do not share its goals see no point in joining it.

The Democrats, in any case, should not tolerate conservatism on the part of their candidates and officeholders—that is, at the level where the party helps elect its nominees and must take responsibility for their public actions. The most flagrant example of this problem is of course the Democratic senator or congressman—usually but not always a southerner—who gets elected on the basis of almost everything the national party opposes. It is unfortunate enough that southern conservatives can still preempt the party label. It is nothing short of scandalous that the national party, after freely lending its name, then allows the Democratic congressional party to reward these Democrats with committee chairmanships. It takes a man of John Kenneth Galbraith's acid humor to do justice to the situation. Every two years, after voting to organize the two houses of Congress, he notes, "the majority of the Party—the modern wing which has long monopolized the Presidential power—places itself under the control of the Southern wing of the Party. The control is exercised by the Southern committee chairmen. Having thus empowered men whose beliefs are wholly at odds with the avowed convictions of the rest of the Party, and who represent a small fraction of its total voting numbers, the Party as a party then dissolves. The Southern leaders form a firm coalition with conservative Republicans for the ensuing two years. The Northern majority then fights the coalition for the same period." And the southerners entrenched in the policymaking and fiscal decisionmaking centers on Capitol Hill, especially when they vote with Republicans, are often more than a match for the divided rank and file congressional liberals.

For southern and other conservatives this is a bountiful arrangement; for all other Democrats it would be uproariously absurd if it were not so tragic in its impact on national policymaking. For the national Democratic party to continue with this system into the 1970s would be cynically dishonest. A party that hands over power to those who oppose its principles is neither morally nor politically fit to govern.

Catering to conservatives is rapidly becoming as politically unrealistic for the Democrats as it is morally wrong. What about the vast numbers of moderates or middle-of-the-roaders who in political outlook now fall between the two parties? Scammon and Wattenberg have reminded us that many of these voters are concerned with old-fashioned economic and newer "social" issues such as crime, race relations, social order, patriotism, campus disorders, and related issues. Certainly the Democrats cannot ignore the genuine problems that are reflected in concern over these issues. Certainly they cannot ignore those whom Scammon and Wattenberg call the "progressive forces of the center." But to adopt moderate positions in order to cater to conservatives on issues such as crime would be to repeat the error the Democrats made in recent years and back in the nineteenth century, when they tried and failed to compete with the Republicans for conservative support. It would be to overplay the economic and social issues and underplay the psychological issues that may well dominate American politics in this decade. It would be to ignore the possibilities of great leadership.

In any case, Democrats face staggering tasks. Stultified by their conservative subparty in Congress and by some of their own procedures, they must plan in terms of a new popular movement that would work through the party and reform it in the process. Now, indeed, is the time for all good men to come to the aid of their party, but to use it, not venerate it. All these tasks will mean a heavy burden for both the movement and the party; at the least it will mean controversy and turmoil as those who believe in the American credo consciously and conspicuously convert the Democracy into a national agency capable of empowering government to carry out the platform of the party.

Still, as John Kennedy used to say, "there is no sense in raising hell and not being successful." The whole point of a hell-raising movement and a rejuvenated party is to attain certain goals. These ends will demand not only transformation of the national government and reform of the party, but a capacity to locate and recruit brilliant, creative leadership in the years ahead.

CHAPTER 9

The Crisis of Leadership

Very occasionally in the life of a nation a long-gathering moral issue explodes on the American scene with such force that old guideposts are knocked askew. Practical politicians long accustomed to trading and brokering in familiar marketplaces suddenly find themselves on strange ground dominated by moralists and visionaries. Negotiation becomes difficult, for those inflamed by the new issues do not want to dicker and chaffer in the old marketplace.

Occasionally too, as in 1917 and 1940, issues of foreign policy become so acute as to override both the familiar economic and the new moral issues at home. The remarkable aspect of American politics today is that all three sets of issues have converged at the same time. Any one of these sets of issues is hard for politicians to deal with; all three would create a crisis of leadership during the best of times. But this is not the best of times for American leaders. The same Gallup poll that found people to be anticipating a breakdown in American society also uncovered a crisis of confidence in the national leadership. As the authors of the survey concluded, such popular anxiety could generate any one of several types of leadership: demogoguery, which would sensationalize the reasons for the anxiety and oversimplify the alternatives at home and abroad; tranquilization, which would invoke old symbols of conservatism and the status quo; or activism, which could respond to and build upon the public's growing awareness of pressing problems. "Leadership both in and out of government—regardless of political persuasion or affiliation—can move ahead of the people," the study concluded, "and take as its keynote the public's sense that new priorities and approaches are needed."

Mass anxieties and leadership failures feed on each other. After long study of the interaction of political activists and the people, V. O. Key concluded that democracies decay not because of the cupidity of the masses but because of the stupidity and self-seeking of leadership echelons. The people "do not corrupt themselves; if they are corrupt, they have been corrupted." Mass pessimism and cynicism, too, reflect a leadership that has lost its nerve.

Many of the young have repudiated American leadership, and indeed even the concept of leadership, just as they have the two major parties and the governmental system. They have seen heroes not much older than themselves assassinated, others jailed, others corrupted, others coopted by the establishment. They are suspicious of charismatic leaders and contemptuous of hucksters and vacillators. For many such reasons, and from a sense of common brotherhood that denies individual competition and superiority, youth groups like SNCC and its successors have eschewed appointed or elected leadership in favor of collective leadership or of none at all.

But no ordered change is possible without leadership. The disenchantment with it is due in part to the notion that leadership is an alien activity conducted by remote elites. In fact leadership can be tamed and directed toward both creative and democratic ends only if it is seated in a system that provides for a crucial role for intellectuals and for popular participation all through the system.

INTELLECTUAL LEADERSHIP

In *La Trahison des Clercs*, Julian Benda concluded that intellectuals had sold out to the practical men of power while still clinging to their status as intellectuals. They had given up detachment for political passion, independence for involvement, the pursuit of truth for the tasting of power. American intellectuals have come under similar charges in recent years as foreign and domestic projects they helped design have failed. They have been accused of putting their special expertness at the service of the power brokers, of forsaking the detachment, the concern for truth, and the devotion to humane values expected of intellectuals at their best.

Overinvolvement with various Establishments has not been the only failing of American intellectuals; the opposite course—militant noncooperation or quiet retreat into ivory towers—has been another. Not only have some intellectuals exhibited in self-imposed exile, at home or abroad, a large measure of purism, sectarianism, and downright snobbery; they have shown a perverse hostility and ignorance toward the political system within which men of affairs have to act. They have dwelt on Utopian goals without any consideration of the means required to reach them, aside from a stock of moral indignation. Hofstadter noted that Henry Adams and many intellectuals of the 1890s had felt disturbed and frustrated, but he doubted that in any age there had been such alienation of the intellectuals as in this one. "There's not much dialogue left in the fashionable intellectual community between those who are alienated from the society and those who are prepared to make an intelligent defense of it. Almost the entire intellectual community is lost in dissent, so to speak. Radicalism is irresistibly chic. . . ."

Few have been the intellectuals in America who understood the need not for rejection of the world of power but for a combination of confrontation of it and involvement with it. "In his search for the truth," said Hans Morgenthau, "the ideal type of intellectual is oblivious to power; in his pursuit of power, the politician at best will use truth as a means to his ends. Yet the two worlds are also potentially intertwined; for truth has a message that is relevant to power, and the very existence of power has a bearing both upon the expression and recognition of truth. The two worlds are not only separate from, and potentially intertwined with each other, they are also hostile to each other. Truth threatens power, and power threatens truth. . . . Power, in order to be effective, must appear as something other than what it actually is. . . . Conversely, truth, by unmasking the pretensions of power, at the very least disturbs the powers-that-be; for it puts power on the intellectual and moral defensive. Furthermore, it questions the purposes and processes of power and thereby endangers the very framework within which power operates. . . ."

But the kind of creativity and innovation that we will desperately need in the years ahead will be impossible without intellectuals who can at one time supply expertise to government and at another criticize government from within, but act at all times with a commitment to certain ends and a detachment from prescribed means; who help elevate the purposes and improve the methods of government, but only for principles which they approve; who, in the old phrase, can think like men of action, and act like men of thought. Sometimes the intellectual will find himself more effective contributing and criticizing from the inside, sometimes from the outside; the test will not be gratifying his instinct for power or his urge to retreat but his capacity to think boldly and critically about the interaction of ends and means.

The most vital function of intellectuals will be as prickers of the balloon of consensus. How many errors have been committed in the name of national unity or bipartisan foreign policy or the doctrine that "politics stops at the water's edge"? Not only does an obsession with consensus make for a flabby government that seeks by conciliation the agreement of all major groups before it acts. It also leads to the branding of opposition as disloyalty. And it deprives government of the challenge and sting of a loyal but pugnacious opposition. The record of American intellectuals in rejecting "unity" is relatively good, perhaps because opposing the herd is congenial to the outsider. The capacity for dissent will be especially valuable in the years ahead when government will be massing its power for the great tasks ahead.

Maintaining the right combination of involvement-and-detachment toward the system calls for unusual qualities. Yet we have a striking example of how a group of intellectuals in the best sense of the word—men interested in ideas both for their own sake and for their social significance—have had an enormous impact on American society. This was the Warren Court. If the justices had been merely men of legal expertise and practical common sense they would not have dared make the sweeping rulings that have made judicial history. On the grounds of practicality and common sense, of accommodation and adjustment, they would have refused to override *Plessy* v. *Ferguson* and the other segregationist rulings; rather they would have tried to modify and reform segregation bit by bit (as they had done in previous rulings). They might have attempted to mediate and compromise on questions of congressional redistricting, racial gerrymandering, rural overrepresentation, the poll tax, discriminatory registration requirements, bias against blacks in the sale of houses, and a host of rights of persons accused of crime. But they did not.

The sweeping decision of the courts in these and other sensitive areas shocked many at the time. But events have vindicated the Court. Only by acting boldly could it hope to keep ahead of public feeling and social eruption. In effect, the Supreme Court experimented with the strategy proposed in this book for social equality and environmental control—the court *nationalized* crucial sectors of the struggle to protect civil liberties and civil rights. It boldly thrust federal power into every state and locality in the nation. The heavens did not fall—neither did the Constitution.

The Warren Court, like other powerholders, learned through painful experience that one-foot-at-a-time gradualism was not enough. The court in the *Brown* case in 1954 issued its historic decision against separate-but-equal, but postponed specific decrees until 1955, as it seemed sensible to give the South a year to prepare for a drastic readjustment. The delay probably was a mistake, as former Justice Black later conceded: it enabled segregationist leaders to rally their cohorts and prepare for battle, strengthened the doubts of Eisenhower fainthearts, confused and discouraged moderate leaders in the South, and gave pause to integrationists everywhere. The court, in retrospect, would have done better to tear the adhesive off the wound quickly rather than by degrees. Later the court was more resolute in school integration decisions and on other issues, as in the one-man, one-vote reapportionment decisions, in which, despite warnings that it would get caught in a political thicket, the court simply made clear that it *meant* one man, one vote, legally and mathematically. Opposition in the state legislatures, ancient citadels of states' rights and state gerrymandering, melted before the display of moral principle, constitutional authority, and political audacity.

The Supreme Court, of course, had a legitimacy and constitutional standing beyond that of any other groups of intellectuals, though it based the *Brown* decision itself on the testimony of social scientists regarding the damaging effects of segregation on children. Still, the Court's moral authority and actual coercive power were by no means unlimited; many doubted that its rulings would be enforced. As things have turned out, the holdings and opinions of the Warren Court are superb examples of uncommon sense. The lesson should not be lost on intellectuals. Whether they frequent the corridors of power, or isolate themselves on a mountaintop, or shuttle back and forth, they are the custodians of truth as they can best discern it, the disturbers of the public peace, the guardians of the unorthodox, the promoters of the novel, the controversial, and the audacious—and always the spokesmen of uncommon sense.

PARTICIPATORY LEADERSHIP

The massing of the political and governmental weight of the nation to overcome priority problems will depend ultimately on popular participation. It has long been accepted that democracy needs a vast number of people who not only vote but man the party and electoral machinery, canvass door to door for votes, write letters to the editor, raise political money, fight for social and civic reform, recruit good men for office, scrutinize the records of their representatives, investigate, monitor, criticize, praise, expose, agitate. These are the practical requirements of a democracy.

But a libertarian democracy should also protect the citizen's effective right *not* to participate in politics, or to participate in ways, at times, and for purposes of his own choosing. "One of the severe totalitarian features of contemporary 'pan-politicalism' is its insistence that politics, at all times and in all places, ought to be the concern of everyone," Peter Berger says. "This great lapse of the imagination is one of the most dubious blessings of modern democracy. It has reached a grotesque climax in the 'participatory' ideal of the contemporary left. It is of fundamental importance to reiterate, in the face of these ideological aberrations, that human life is infinitely richer in its possibilities of fulfillment than in its political expressions, and that it is indeed a basic human right to live apolitically—a right that may be denied only for the most urgent reasons." For some persons participation in itself is a proximate if not an ultimate end; they realize themselves in the excitement and fulfillment of active politics. But for others participation is but a means to an end, and that end may be to live in a representative democracy where one can shun politics without feeling that the representative system will wither away. During the war Franklin D. Roosevelt wrote Harry Hopkins that he had had a grand time in a vacation retreat—"slept twelve hours out of the twenty-four, sat in the sun, never lost my temper, and decided to let the world go hang. The interesting thing is that the world didn't hang." Sometimes the citizen, too, can let the world go hang. It all depends, as Berger says further, on "what 'they' are doing—and, needless to say, on what 'we' propose to do instead."

Still, we must not set up an ideal of nonparticipation either. What democracy requires seems to be neither a great mass of people intensely involved in politics—such a condition might be too volatile and volcanic for its delicate institutions—but a range of intensity of political activity. Political analysts have found such a range in the United States: less than one percent of Americans run for office or solicit party funds, and only four or five percent become active party members or attend party meetings, but ten percent or more give money, wear a button, or put a sticker on their car, twenty-five to thirty percent try to talk others into voting a certain way, and forty to seventy percent expose themselves to political stimuli and/or vote. These degrees of participation tend to increase in presidential campaigns and decrease in state and local.

This intensity of participation is doubtless too low, but the vitality of democracy probably depends less on the number of activists than on the vigorous interaction of leaders and led throughout the whole system. The leaders arouse the followers, stimulate them to action, satisfy or disappoint them; the people variously empower their leaders, retain them, oppose them, dethrone them. This process goes on at every level of electoral, party, and group politics. Thus is created a structure of leadership in which most of us are both leaders and followers, shifting from one to the other as our roles and relations change. All this is the essence of participatory leadership.

Participatory leadership at the top levels of the political party can have a special safeguard role in the years ahead. In the aftermath of Vietnam and other foreign and domestic failures of presidential leadership, Americans are fearful of untrammeled presidential power in foreign policy and warmaking. Congress has, generally, failed to check the president's warmaking power, and in any event cannot act in the early hours of crisis. The loyal party opposition has failed to oppose, largely because of bipartisan understandings about "adjourning politics in time of national crisis." The checks and balances do not operate because crisis usually produces a sharp if fleeting solidarity in the otherwise divided political system. The men who can best help restrain and steady a president's hand during crises are not his political enemies in Congress or the opposition party but his political friends who are personally loyal to him but who have political perspectives and bases somewhat detached from those of the White House. The best organized device for stabilizing presidential power is a small party council of persons who have a commitment to party goals and promises, a national outlook, the experience of long-term collaboration with the president and other leaders, access to the president, and the capacity both to sustain him and to confront and challenge him, as allies in a common cause.

The recruitment of leadership is a vital link in this whole process. In the American individualistic society we are used to ambitious men acting on their own, vaulting into the political arena, battling their way to the top, winning power to a large extent over the heads of the people. All too rarely do we—even the activists among us—search out potential leaders, enlist them, and help them gain office. The delegation of good citizens marching to a man's home to urge him to give himself to the nation's or the community's welfare is usually a figment of the official campaign biography. But recruitment is participatory leadership at its best because it involves people in leader selection at the start rather than being presented with unsatisfactory choices later. It is one of the most rewarding and underestimated political opportunities for rank-and-file activists today.

It is an opportunity that may be enlarged, at least at the presidential level. One effect of recent reforms in the method of choosing convention delegates will be to enable voters to take a more direct and active part than before in getting their favorites on the ballot as candidates for president, and themselves on the ballot as candidates for convention delegate. Only two or three steps are typically required—getting a few hundred signatures in order to gain a place on the presidential primary ballot as candidates for delegate, linking oneself to the candidacy of a presidential aspirant, and mobilizing voters directly for the latter. The possibilities here of participatory leadership are almost limitless. While opening up presidential primaries in this manner may produce fragmentation and even chaos in the presidential nomination process, it does enormously augment the prospects of recruiting candidates and building a cadre directly in support of them.

We must concede, however, that the range of participatory leadership has proved inadequate in a nation where thirty or forty percent of eligible voters never vote and over half fail to vote in most state and local elections. In any democracy there will always be a "hard core of chronic know-nothings" beyond enticement into the political arena by even the most tempting methods. But thirty or forty million Americans completely closed off from the political struggle is as indefensible as the almost equal number who live below the poverty line—and of course many of these millions are the same. To involve most of these people in politics is the task of officeholders, civic leaders, parents, registration officials—the task of all of us. But the main burden will fall on the national political system and on presidential leadership. Ultimately many of these millions of nonparticipants can be involved by parties offering real alternatives and exciting battles, and by heroic, controversial candidates—by candidates, as someone said of Huey Long, with a "kindlin' power."

PRESIDENTIAL LEADERSHIP

Every commencement speech, at least in the old days, urged the graduates to lead—it was not always clear where to. While leadership is imperative, especially in a democracy, general exhortations to leadership blur the focused responsibility that is also vital to a democracy. Hence we must think in terms of specific leaders.

The leader can be only the elected leader of all of us, the president. The ponderous and fragmented governmental system cannot begin to attack the priority tasks without constant pressure and heavy repeated pushes from the top. Disenchantment with the failures of four administrations in Indochina must not blind us to the absolute necessity of extraordinary presidential leadership during this decade. Not only must the president move skillfully hour to hour through his many roles as chief legislator, chief executive, chief propagandist, and all the rest. He must be a heroic leader who can involve people and not merely preach to them, a man of rare uncommon sense as well as practicality. He must be a principled, committed leader in domestic policy and affairs, a prudent and innovative manager in foreign affairs. He must be a good planner, able to direct not a planned society but a planning society; he must also be a resourceful day-to-day improviser within his planning. He must know how to hoard and enhance his presidential and personal power, how to guard his reputation as politician in chief, how to keep his options as wide and open as possible, how to manipulate and bargain and conciliate and adjust—and yet do all this without succumbing to operationalism for its own sake or becoming in the eyes of the press and the people merely a master wheeler-dealer, or manipulator in chief.

But we will need much more than all this in the man who will preside over this decade. We need a president who will change the institutional structure around him because he will see that he cannot achieve his goals within it, and who will understand what changing this structure means. It means organizing a new popular movement of people who would join with most of the present Democratic party rank and file to create a genuine national party that could elect creative leaders to office and then sustain and steady them during their years of governance. It means ruling in partnership with Congress if national goals can thus be met, but acting without Congress if the national legislature is unable to come to grips with the job ahead. It means making the White House an effective planning agency as well as an action agency. It means a reorganization and rejuvenation of the executive branch so that administrative power can be focused and applied through flexible task forces with specific priority goals, and within a relatively brief span of time. It means the transformation of state and local government to the extent necessary to work with the national government to achieve national priorities.

Within the political system the presidency is, actually and symbolically, the apex of power. When its power is exercised most responsibly it is not confined to mere tinkering, mere management, absorption in means without concern for ends. Its concept of office is inclusive; its planning is overarching. This is by no means to say that it draws under governmental control all aspects of American life—such attempts at control reflect presidential weakness not strength. But it is to say that the presidency at its best seeks to liberate American society as a whole from whatever binds it. It seeks to extend the theory and the practice of equality. It inspires the people as a whole, as Franklin Roosevelt did in the early New Deal, transforming fears and selfishness into confidence and generosity. It rallies and coordinates a broadly based coalition of concern—in business, labor, the professions, and other private institutions. It defines the national priorities, invests its resources in accordance with those definitions, and cajoles and prods reluctant public and private institutions to serve those priorities. It uses its vast authority and funds for the broadest social purposes.

Timing, as well as consistency in purpose, will be an important but puzzling factor in the political equation of a truly effective president. The practical politician has learned, in the vicissitudinous arena of American politics, to seize the first opportunity to run for office and win; to delay is to miss an opportunity that might never reappear. And only in office, says the realist, can he really help people. But what is good for a politician may not be good for the cause. And the manner in which a man runs for office—the commitments he makes, the support he arouses, the kind of victory he wins—affects what he can do in that office. The urgent question is whether a party (or a candidate) should wait

until it can win not merely office but *power* on its own terms—
that is, on the terms of being able to put its program through.
This question cannot be answered abstractly but only on the basis
of the concrete situation existing at the moment. It can be a difficult one. One of the great strategic problems facing the Labor
party in Britain was whether the Laborites would do better to take
office in the 1920s and share power with Liberals or other third
parties, or whether it should resist the temptation of office, build
up its strength, and form a government only when it had its own
parliamentary majority and could put through its own program.
The Democratic party in this country faces much the same question, though in different form. It must make of itself not only a
vehicle to beat Republicans but one to *govern*.

These theoretical problems pose practical dilemmas for candidates. A candidate specifically attempting to uproot an incumbent
president, as the Democrats were required to do in 1972, needed
to show a capacity to develop a personal following that would be
willing later to work within the Democratic party movement,
whether for himself or for some other nominee. He needed, first,
to demonstrate enough strength among Democrats and independents to show well in presidential primaries in the states that have
them, and enough bargaining power and skill to win support
from party leaders in nonprimary states. He needed to maintain
his standing as a national oracle while darting in and out of stores
and union halls in quick hand-shaking tours of key areas. The
problem would be compounded for any man who won the presidential nomination without having established a robust and exten-
sive personal following, as in the case of Adlai Stevenson in 1952.
Then the nominee in the few weeks between the convention and
the start of the battle with the Republicans would be required
to undertake the immense task of almost instant campaign organization. He could not depend on the party-in-being, as John Kennedy discovered in 1960 and Hubert Humphrey in 1968.

No one can blueprint the strategy of the next president but some
issues can be anticipated. No leader who moves ahead audaciously

can expect Congress to support him with enthusiasm, except in a crisis situation like that of 1933, in which case the support from Capitol Hill would be short-lived. The president will have to lead the legislature with weapons more effective than the "blarney, boodle, and bludgeon" with which Kennedy tried to influence his Congress. The president's principal weapons will be his stand on principle—and the people who will back him because he *is* standing on principle. It also seems likely that a president undertaking the drastic innovations required in government in the 1970s cannot escape resistance from a federal judiciary well stocked with Nixon appointees. Opposition to the new president from Congress or the courts could precipitate a constitutional crisis rivaling the famous collision between Franklin Roosevelt and the anti-New Deal Supreme Court of the mid 1930s. In that event the president in the 1970s could learn from history. He would be better advised to make an issue of obstruction and take it openly to the people in a reelection campaign than to attempt the disingenuous court-packing in the name of efficiency that Roosevelt gambled on in 1937. For if means and ends are truly implicit in each other, a leader must take his institutional reforms as well as his goals to the people.

The great political leader is not content to whittle down his goals to what he thinks he can achieve through the existing structure of political forces. Rather he seeks to enlarge and vivify the structure so that the goals can be realized as fully as possible. He knows that archaic governmental routines cannot always be broken up by adjustment and adaptation but, as Burnham says, by "the application of overwhelming external force." Only the president can apply such force within the government. But he cannot fundamentally alter means unless he is acting in terms of some end, purpose, or doctrine. "Those who are possessed of a definite body of doctrine," Winston Churchill said, "and of deeply rooted convictions on it will be in a much better position to deal with the shifts and surprises of daily affairs than those who are merely taking short views, and indulging their natural impulses as they are evoked by what they read from day to day." The next president need not be a man of ideology, saintliness, or charisma; he must be a man of doctrine, principle, and purpose.

THE PRESIDENT AS WORLD LEADER

The president can "never again be the mere domestic figure he has been throughout so large a part of our history," Woodrow Wilson said in 1907. The other nations of the world look askance on America, "half in envy, half in fear, and wonder with a deep anxiety what she will do with her vast strength. . . . Our President must always, henceforth, be one of the great powers of the world, whether he acts greatly or wisely or not."

The American president has no choice whether or not to be a world leader. The expectation of the nations of the world and the structure of the government he heads compel him to lead. But whether he acts "greatly or wisely or not" *is* a matter of option and decision, as well as of contingency and luck. Some presidents, forced suddenly into a role of leadership in a world crisis, have responded with a fine grasp of the realities and a deep concern for American ideals. Others have substituted moralisms or expediency for principled realism. In a world of incessant and often calamitous change, are there any guidelines to presidential leadership that will avoid the pitfalls of rigid dogma and yet keep the nation on a course consistent with its deepest values?

Given the fragmented structure of world politics, certain rules of thumb can be useful while all general rules and dogmas must be suspect. "The ideological decontamination of conventional foreign policy is a precondition of an American foreign policy that is both peaceful and successful," Morgenthau says. "This has always been so; for accommodation and compromise, which are the aims of diplomacy, are incompatible with the contest of political ideologies, each claiming a monopoly of wisdom and virtue and trying to transform the world in its image. Foreign policies seeking the triumph of one political ideology at the expense of another have always issued in particularly fanatical and bloody wars, which have been inconclusive to boot unless they physically limited the supporters of one ideology altogether." Survival in the years ahead will depend less on set principles and more on understandings, expectations, *le sens de l'état*—a sense of the web of authority and the strands of action—in short, on an uncommon degree of common sense.

The test is whether a president and a nation can support deeply humanist principles ᵗhat are good for mankind without violating the rights of others or increasing the danger of war. The only kind of intervention that can strengthen liberty and equality is the kind of intervention that aids those who wish to be free and those determined to be equal. Economic intervention, whether in the form of aid or deprivation, has proved to be no panacea; it too must be used selectively, with no expectation of assured compliance, domestic reform, political stability—or gratitude.

Intervention abroad must be neither flatly adopted nor flatly rejected as a principle. Nor should nonintervention, which can itself be a form of intervention. These are means only and must serve worthy ends. We must cast off our most dangerous inheritance from the Vietnam period—the notion that since protracted war with mixed results will always be unpopular with the American people, we must in the future either intervene quickly and decisively with all the power we can mobilize or else refrain from world leadership altogether. The decision to intervene should be made on the basis of a sophisticated knowledge of the facts and their implications for the security of the United States. Our leadership must recognize that leaving power voids can be as dangerous as trying to fill them; witness what happened in Korea after we pulled out following the World War II occupation. Intervention must be employed variously, flexibly, according to intention, scope, type of involvement, its positive or negative purpose, and of course its effect on allies and adversaries. We must recognize that intervention is a highly limited and unpredictable weapon. Only full-scale intervention—that is, occupation—can achieve such broad aims as fundamental political reform of the occupied countries, as the experience of postwar Germany and Japan suggests. But such intervention is a desperate last resort in a situation highly dangerous to the United States, and the occasion may never again arise in a world where general war threatens survival itself. Intervention must be genuinely collective for the sake of legitimacy and moderation, through the agencies of world law in so far as possible.

Of our leaders we must expect neither too much nor too little—but as a minimum we have a right to expect that the avoidance of a nuclear war will be the president's most important single aim. To achieve this paramount purpose he must understand the world as it is and not behave as though it was already the world he would prefer it to be. Nor should he seek to compel it to change simply to suit his nation's desires. In maintaining the security of the nation and preserving its libertarian and egalitarian institutions, war—any kind of war—must be a dire last resort, and the objective must be not to "win" it but to contain, contract, and end it promptly. These would seem to be commonplaces—but how often have these commonplaces been commonplace?

The president's most creative role would be to take the lead in building up a wide variety of supranational institutions that might ultimately foster on a world scale the freedoms he supports at home. The building of a genuine global federalism or world government cannot come soon, for it will depend on the weaving of a close web of political, economic, and cultural links across nations. But it must come.

The president can see that his own country does not disgrace the values the nation represents abroad. "The way in which Americans live, the quality of American life, is the most important aspect of American foreign policy today," according to Robert F. Byrnes. ". . . The democratic and, above all, the open way in which we have faced our social and economic problems has been the most impressive and influential aspect of American foreign policy, not only in dealing with the Soviet Union but in our relations with other peoples of the world." This has little to do with American security; it has much to do with the moral worth of the American society and the standard it *could* set for the world. Thus presidential leadership can demand that the United States government set a standard for civility in its attitude toward the rest of the world—and toward its own people. Such a standard would require that the government abandon the arrogance of power and the myth of American omnipotence; that it recognize and tolerate diversity in the world; that it share with its citizens the rationale and the means proposed for foreign policy; that it tone down its rhetoric and, in many situations, lower its profile; that, on Dean Acheson's advice, it forswear bullying, taking advantage of the hardship of others to drive political bargains, lying or boasting, sanctimonious lecturing of others on their faults, or thanking of God that we are not as other men.

Just as American values have a positive thrust in domestic policy, so they have more than a negative dimension in world leadership. All in the name of realism and practicality America has helped to sustain dictatorship and has neglected those peoples who are struggling to achieve self-determination after generations of colonial exploitation and neglect. This chapter of our foreign policy is largely closed, since most colonial peoples have won political independence, but the principle remains: to what degree will we help sustain those peoples seeking the same values of liberty and equality that we cherish? The American Declaration of Independence is cited and copied throughout the emerging countries. Its precepts have proved contagious. At the very least, American world leadership should so act as not to dishonor the ideas it has given to the world; at the most, it should act so as to help make them a reality. But, paradoxically, this cannot be forced upon others; each people must make its own independence, achieve its own liberty and equality.

So world leadership is neither a crusade nor a cop-out; it is a deft and restrained mingling of many methods and policies to improve the chances of liberty and equality in all nations. In a situation where means dominate ends, perhaps what we do is often less important than how we do it. As Lord David Cecil said about Joseph Conrad's view of life, "What one lives for may be uncertain. How one lives is not. . . . Man should live nobly though he does not see any practical reason for it, simply because in the mysterious inexplicable mixture of beauty and ugliness, virtue and baseness in which he finds himself he must want to be on the side of the beautiful and the virtuous." That is the most uncommon common sense of all.

As we face the 1970s our thoughts go back two hundred years to a time when giants seemed to have sprung out of the soil of the little colonies clinging to the Atlantic seaboard. Giants they seemed then—giants they seem today, as we study their lives, acknowledge their shortcomings, but marvel at their capacity to shake off rule from overseas and then to establish it brilliantly in their own new nation. Is it conceivable that in the last third of this century, in another time of great peril and great opportunity, we can generate the same kind of uncommon leadership? The historical record—the fact that crises have produced the Jacksons, Lincolns, Roosevelts, Kennedys—would indicate that we can. The problem, as this book seeks to show, will not be leadership, the availability of great talent, but the institutions that thwart and crush it, and the opportunism and false realism that demean it.

At the end of his monumental study of America and its dilemma, Gunnar Myrdal asked leave to close with a personal note. Studying human beings, he said, was not discouraging. When he recalled "the long gallery of persons whom, in the course of this inquiry, he has come to know with the impetuous but temporary intimacy of the stranger—sharecroppers and plantation owners, workers and employers, merchants and bankers, intellectuals, preachers, organization leaders, political bosses, gangsters, black and white, men and women, young and old, southerners and northerners—the general observation retained is the following: Behind all outward dissimilarities, behind their contradictory valuations, rationalizations, vested interests, group allegiances and animosities, behind fears and defense constructions, behind the role they play in life and the mask they wear, people are all much alike on a fundamental level. And they are all good people. They want to be rational and just. They all plead to their conscience that they meant well even when things went wrong." The question was why good people so often made life a hell for themselves and each other when they lived together in a family, community, nation, or world.

The remedy is the same as in 1776 and 1787—to rediscover our overarching values, to recommit ourselves to them, to restructure our institutions to fulfill them, and to support and sustain leaders who will serve them. Who will emerge as the Franklin, Washington, Jefferson, Adams, or Madison of our time?

Author's Note

I am grateful to Jeannette Hopkins, of Harper & Row, who made substantial and indispensable intellectual as well as editorial contributions to this book; to Benjamin Baker, Ramsey Clark, Charles Frankel, and Adam Yarmolinsky, who generously took time from their demanding lives to write detailed critiques of the first draft of the manuscript; to my son Stewart, who pointedly criticized the chapter on revolution from his experience as a resistance activist, and to Jay Fahn, who reviewed it from his somewhat different perspective as a member of the same generation; and above all to my wife, who brought a keen and experienced editorial eye to the manuscript as well as unfailing support and encouragement to the author.

J. M. B.

Reference and Subject Index

This index refers to both subjects and bibliographical sources. Page numbers in *italics* refer to pages in sources cited; page numbers in roman type refer to pages in *Uncommon Sense*.

Acheson, Dean, "Morality, Moralism, and Diplomacy," *The Yale Review*, June 1958, *p. 493*: 179
Adams, Henry, 164
Adams, John, 36
Adams, John Quincy, 36
Administrative task force, 128, 137
Advisory Commission on Intergovernmental Relations, *Urban and Rural America: Policies for Future Growth* (Washington: Government Printing Office, 1968), 87–88
Allen, Frederick Lewis, *The Big Change* (New York: Harper & Brothers, 1952), *p. 286*: 30
American ideology, *see* Ideology, American
American system, 3–15
  rejection of, 56–58, 61; *see also* Revolution
Anti-domino dogma, 49–50
Anti-patriotism dogma, 51
Anti-presidential power dogma, 53–54
Apter, David, "Ideology and Discontent," in David Apter, ed., *Ideology and Discontent* (Glen-coe, Ill.: Free Press, 1964), quoted in Walter Dean Burnham, *Critical Elections and the Mainsprings of American Politics* (New York: W. W. Norton, 1970), *pp. 137, 139*: 142–143
Arendt, Hannah, interview by Adelbert Reif, *The New York Review*, Apr. 22, 1971, *p. 10*: 59
Army Corps of Engineers, 127
Ash, Roy, "The Government Needs an Overhaul," *The New York Times*, Mar. 25, 1971, *p. 39*: 127
Attica prison riot, ix, 118
Auden, W. H., 11

Baker, Benjamin, correspondence with author, Aug. 1971, 137
Beliefs, 92–110; *see also* Ideology, American
Benda, Julian, *La Trahison des Clercs* (Paris: Bernard Grosset, 1927), 164
Berger, Peter L., and Richard J. Neuhaus, *Movement and Revolution* (Garden City, N.Y.: Doubleday & Co., 1970), *p. 16*:

168; *see also* Neuhaus, Richard J.

Berkeley Liberation Committee, program: *Oakland Tribune,* June 5, 1969, quoted in Zbigniew Brzezinski, *Between Two Ages* (New York: Viking Press, 1970), *p. 232:* 65–66

Berrigan, Daniel, S.J., interview by Robert Coles, *The New York Review,* Mar. 11, 1971, *p. 10:* 61–63

Bettelheim, Bruno, 57

Black, Hugo, 167

Black militants, 69–70

Black Muslims, 71

Black Panthers, 69–70

Black Power, 66, 70, 73

Black Power Conference, 68

Black Power manifesto, 66

Blacks, 6, 18
  African homeland proposed, 68
  civil rights, 25–30
  in class system, 142
  discrimination against, government policies, 23–25
  Eisenhower and, 25–26
  equality of, 100, 102
  fraternity as ideal, 105
  freedmen after Civil War, 21–22
  inequality of, 83
  Johnson's program, 28
  Kennedy's program, 26–28
  in labor unions, 150
  Lincoln and, 20–22
  lynching, legislation against, 24
  march on Washington, 1941, proposed, 24–25
  march on Washington, 1963, 27–28
  moral issue of, 19
  Myrdal's principle of cumulation, 84–85
  Nixon's policy, 28–29
  partitioning of U.S. proposed, 68
  presidential policies on, 22–30
  as revolutionaries, 57, 66–71, 73
  riots, 18, 69, 87, 89
  Roosevelt, F. D., and, 24–25
  Roosevelt, T., and, 22–23
  school integration, busing, 29

separate-but-equal formula, 117
separatism, 68
slavery, 19–21
  in suburbs, 131, 141
  as voters, 141–142, 144–145, 150, 154–155
  Wilson and, 23–24

Braden, William, *The Age of Aquarius* (Chicago: Quadrangle Books, 1970), *p. 69:* 57–58

Brogan, Denis W., 98

Brown, H. Rap, in Peter L. Berger and Richard J. Neuhaus, *Movement and Revolution* (New York: Doubleday & Co., 1970), *p. 109:* 69

Brown v. Board of Education, 166–167

Bryce, James, 98

Brzezinski, Zbigniew, *Between Two Ages: America's Role in the Technetronic Era* (New York: The Viking Press, 1970), *p. 195:* 10

Burnham, Walter Dean, *Critical Elections and the Mainsprings of American Politics* (New York: W. W. Norton, 1970), *Chap. 5:* 140; *p. 92:* 147; *p. 183:* 175

Burns, James MacGregor: on foreign policy: *Presidential Government* (Boston: Houghton Mifflin Co., 1966), *pp. 269–270:* 41

  on Roosevelt: *Roosevelt: The Soldier of Freedom* (New York: Harcourt Brace Jovanovich, 1970), *pp. 549–550:* 38–39

Byrnes, Robert F., testimony before the Subcommittee on National Security and International Operations, Committee on Government Operations, U.S. Senate, 92nd Congress, 1st Sess., Part 5, Apr. 2, 1971, *p. 132:* 178–179

Califano, Joseph, *The Student Revolution* (New York: W. W. Norton, 1970), *pp. 41–43:* 65

Calley, William, ix
Cambodia, 46
Carswell, G. Harrold, 29
Cecil, Lord David, quoted in Dean
   Acheson, "Morality, Moralism,
   and Diplomacy," *The Yale Re-
   view*, June 1958, *p. 493:* 180
Central Intelligence Agency (CIA),
   36
Change, 77–91
   cumulation, theory of, 84–87
   directed, 7, 14
   government in, 77–80, 86–89
   poverty and, 78–79, 86
   priorities in, 13–14
   reform and, 81–83
   strategies in, 14–15
Chavez, César, 71
China, Roosevelt's policy on, 38–39
China, Communist, 41, 50, 104–105
   in Korean war, 43, 52
   Nixon's visit to, 48
   Soviet Union and, 51–52
   U.S. foreign relations, 53
   in Vietnam war, 44, 52
Churchill, Winston, in W. W. Ros-
   tow, "The Planning of Foreign
   Policy" (Baltimore: School of
   Advanced International Studies,
   Johns Hopkins University),
   175–176
CIA (Central Intelligence Agency),
   36
Cities: government, 130–131; *see
   also* Government, localization of
   national, 131, 138
   suburbs, 131, 141
Civil rights and civil liberties, 121
   Congress obstructs legislation, 23–
   25, 27–28, 119, 124
   presidential programs, 25–30
   revolutionary attitude toward, 64–
   65, 67
Civil service, recommendation on,
   128–129
Civil War, 144
   freedom after, 21–22
   Lincoln on, 20–22
Clark, Kenneth B.: *Dark Ghetto*
   (New York: Harper & Row,
   1965), 102

Youth in the Ghetto (New York:
   Harlem Youth Opportunities,
   Unlimited, Inc., 1964), 102
Classes, social, 142–143
Cloward, Richard, and Lloyd E.
   Ohlin, *Delinquency and Oppor-
   tunity: A Theory of Delinquent
   Gangs* (New York: Free Press,
   1966), 102
Colombia, 38
Columbia University disorders, 70
Common Cause, 141
Common sense, 5, 8, 19
Communes, 71–72
Communism: containment of, 50–51
   monolithic, 41, 51
   no-monolith dogma, 51–53
Communist party, 68
Congress, 7–8
   civil rights measures in, 23–25, 27–
   28, 119, 124
   Democratic party in, 140, 159–
   160
   filibuster, 119, 124
   House Rules Committee, 116, 119
   Joint Economic Committee, 123
   Kennedy and, 27–28, 32, 175
   parties in, 124–125, 146–147
   powers of, 115–116, 119
   president and, 53, 124–125, 172,
   175
   in Reconstruction period, 22
   reform, proposals, 124–126
   veto power, 119, 125
Conquest, Robert, testimony before
   the Subcommittee on National
   Security of the Committee on
   Government Operations, U.S.
   Senate, 92nd Cong., 1st Sess.,
   Part 6, Apr. 30, 1971, *p. 188:*
   52
Consciousness III, 59
Conservatism: in Democratic party,
   159–160
   economic issues and, 16–17
   of government, 118–121
Conservative party, 142
Constitution of France, 1791, Declaration of Rights, 98
Constitution of the United States, 5,
   114–115, 129

Constitution (*cont'd*)
  First Amendment freedoms, 107
  liberty in, 96
  slavery in, 20
Containment of communism, 50–51
Council of Economic Advisers, 123
Crèvecoeur, Hector St. John, 98
Cuba, 38, 40, 50
Cumulation, theory of, 84–87
Czechoslovakia, 40, 42, 54
  Soviet invasion of, 43, 52

Dahl, Robert, *After the Revolution*
    (New Haven: Yale University
    Press, 1930), *p. 105*: 104
Daley, Richard J., 140, 156
Declaration of Independence, 115,
    179
  liberty in, 96, 98
  slavery reference deleted, 19–20
Democratic party, 8, 143, 146–149,
    152–153, 157–161, 172, 174
  blacks and, 141–142
  in cities, 142
  in Congress, 140, 159–160
  conservatism in, 159–160
  convention, 1968, in Chicago, 147,
    157
  history of, 144–145
  platform of 1968, 126
  reform, record of, 157–158
  weakness of, 140, 155–156
Dewey, John, 9–10
Dogmas in foreign policy: anti-
    domino, 49–50
  anti-patriotism, 51
  anti-presidential power, 53–54
  no-monolith, 51–53
Dominican Republic, U.S. policy,
    37, 38
Domino theory, 49–50
Douglas, Paul H., 88
Draper, Theodore, in Richard M.
    Pfeffer, ed., *No More Vietnams?*
    (New York: Harper & Row,
    1968), *p. 29*: 43
Du Bois, W. E. B., 23
Dulles, John Foster, 42, 50
Dutton, Frederick G., *Changing
    Sources of Power* (New York:

McGraw-Hill Book Co., 1971),
    p. 16: 139

Economic progress, 16–19
  presidency and, 30–32
Eisenhower, Dwight D., 102
  and civil rights, 25–26
  foreign policy, 50
Electoral College, 119
Employment Act of 1946, 123
Ends and means, 10
  in foreign policy, 34–42, 48–49,
    54–55
  in government, 113, 117, 135–136
  in ideology, 108–109
  liberal and conservative, 16–17
  in revolution, 60, 63, 65–68
  in transformation of government,
    113
  in Vietnam war, 47–48
Environment: government action on,
    89–90
  as priority, 14, 121
Equality: of condition, 102–104
  inequality and, 82–83, 99–100
  in liberty, 98–103
  liberty in, 95–97
  of opportunity, 99–102
  as priority, 13
  values of, 103–105
Executive branch, reform of, 126–129

Fair Deal, 98
Fair Employment Practices Commit-
    tee (FEPC), 25
Federal Bureau of Investigation
    (FBI), 127
Fischer, John, "Planning for the Sec-
    ond America," *Harper's Mag-
    azine,* Nov. 1969, *p. 21*: 123
Foreign policy, 34–55
  containment in, 50–51
  dogmas, 48–54; *see also* Dogmas
    in foreign policy
  ends and means, 34–42, 48–49,
    54–55
  of presidents, 36–40, 122, 169,
    176–179
  in Vietnam war, 42–49, 54–55,
    122
  after World War II, 40–42

Forman, Charles, 66
Founding Fathers, 5, 19
Four Freedoms, 39, 97–98
Franco, Francisco, 36
Frankel, Charles, in Herman D.
    Stein, ed., *Social Theory and
    Social Invention* (Cleveland:
    Press of Case–Western Reserve
    University, 1968), *p. 20*: 95
Frankel, Max, "Revenue Sharing Is a
    Counterrevolution," *The New
    York Times Magazine*, Apr. 25,
    1971, *p. 28*: 130
Franklin, Benjamin, 9
Fraternity, ideal of, 105
Freedmen after Civil War, 21–22
Freedom, *see* Liberty
French Constitution of 1791, Dec-
    laration of Rights, 98
French Revolution, 105

Galbraith, John Kenneth, "Who
    Needs the Democrats?" *Har-
    per's Magazine*, July 1970, *p.
    53*: 160
Gallup Survey, *The New York Times*,
    June 27, 1971, *pp. 1, 37*: 3,
    162–163
Gardner, John, 141
Garvey, Marcus, 68
Gelb, Leslie, "Today's Lessons from
    the Pentagon Papers," *Life*,
    Sept. 17, 1971, *p. 35*: 44
Geneva agreement on Vietnam, 45
Germany, 178
Germany, East, 51
Ghetto riots, 18, 69, 87, 89
Gilligan, John J., *The New York
    Times*, Nov. 23, 1968, *p. 63*:
    149
Goldwater, Barry, 32, 142
Government: administrative task
    force, 128, 137
    advisory and participatory groups
    in, 136
    agencies, reorganization of, 123,
    126–127
    changes, responsibility for, 77–80,
    86–89
    civil service, recommendations on,
    128–129

conservatism of, 118–121
in Constitution, 114–115
executive branch, 126–129; *see
    also* Presidency
failure, reasons for, 7–10
fragmentation of, 114–118, 120–
    121
liberty and, 96–97, 103
Lincoln on object of, 102
local, 121, 130–135
localization of, 129–138
opportunity programs, 101–103
progress and, 16–33
reform (nationalization), propos-
    als, 121–129
regional agencies proposed, 132–
    138
transformation of, 113–138
Great Britain: civil service, 128
    Labor party, 174
Great Society, 98
Greece, 42
Greeley, Horace, 21
Groups, power, 119–120

Hacker, Andrew, *Newsweek*, July 6,
    1970, *p. 25*: 11
Haiti, 38
Harbaugh, William Henry, *Power
    and Responsibility* (New York:
    Farrar, Straus and Cudahy,
    1961), *p. 522*: 37
Harrington, Michael, "Don't Form
    a Fourth Party; Form a New
    First Party," *The New York
    Times Magazine*, Sept. 13, 1970,
    p. 38: 153
Hartz, Louis, 93
HARYOU study, 102
Haynsworth, Clement, 29
Hilliard, David, in Zbigniew Brze-
    zinski, *Between Two Ages*
    (New York: Viking Press,
    1970), *p. 230*: 69–70
Hitler, Adolf, 39, 97
Hofstadter, Richard, 93
    on intellectuals: in *Newsweek*,
    July 6, 1970, *pp. 21–22*: 164
Hook, Sidney, "John Dewey and
    His Critics," *The New Republic*,
    June 3, 1931, *pp. 73–74*: 10

Hoover, Herbert, 78
  American Individualism (Garden City, N.Y.: Doubleday, Page and Co., 1922), *p. 9*: 100–101
  quoted in Richard Hofstadter, *The American Political Tradition* (New York: Alfred A. Knopf, 1948), *p. 294*: 101
Hopkins, Harry L., 168
Humphrey, Hubert, 142, 147, 174
Hungary, 40, 42, 52

Idealism, distrust of, 9, 92
Ideology, American, 92–110
  equality in liberty, 98–103
  liberty in equality, 95–98
  pragmatism, 93, 108
  values as guides to action, 105–110
  values of liberty and equality, 103–105
Income distribution, 30
India, 39
Individuality as value, 105
Inequality: equalitarian doctrines and, 99–100
  poverty and, 82–83
Inflation, 17
Innis, Roy, 67
Intellectual leadership, 164–167

Jackson, Andrew, 144, 146, 153
Jackson, George, 71
James, William, 9
Japan, 36, 178
Jefferson, Thomas, 141, 145, 146, 148, 153
  on Constitution: in Alpheus T. Mason, *The Supreme Court: Palladium of Freedom* (Ann Arbor: University of Michigan Press, 1962), *p. 10*: 114
  Declaration of Independence, draft of, 19–20, 98
  political party, Republicans, 143–144
  on slavery: in John M. Blum et al., *The National Experience* (New York: Harcourt, Brace & World, 1963), *p. 205*: 20

  on slavery: in Nathan Schachner, *Thomas Jefferson* (New York: Thomas Yoseloff, 1951), *p. 134*: 19–20
Johnson, James Weldon, in Gunnar Myrdal, *An American Dilemma* (New York: Harper & Brothers, 1944), *p. 808*: 68
Johnson, Lyndon B., 6, 31, 87, 88, 123, 153
  civil rights program, 28
  foreign policy, 50
  Vietnam policy, 46
  War on Poverty, 17, 28, 79, 102

Keniston, Kenneth, *Young Radicals: Notes on Committed Youth* (New York: Harcourt, Brace & World, 1968), *p. 260*: 58
Kennan, George, *Memoirs* (Boston: Little, Brown, 1967), 50
Kennedy, John F., 6, 31–32, 55, 123, 145, 147, 153, 174
  and civil rights, 26–28
  on civil rights: in Arthur M. Schlesinger, Jr., *A Thousand Days* (Boston: Houghton Mifflin Company, 1965), *p. 929*: 26
  and Congress, 27–28, 32, 175
  and electoral system, 119
  foreign policy, 50
  poverty program, 79, 102
  quoted in James L. Sundquist, *Politics and Policy* (Washington: The Brookings Institution, 1968), *p. 479*: 161
  "Speeches, Remarks, Press Conferences, and Statements of Senator John F. Kennedy, Aug. 1 through Nov. 7, 1960," *Final Report of the Senate Committee on Commerce*, 87th Cong., 1st Sess., 1961, *p. 904*: 26
Kent State University, 118
Key, V. O., Jr., *Public Opinion and American Democracy* (New York: Alfred A. Knopf, 1961), *pp. 557–558, 561*: 163
Keynes, John Maynard, in Michael Harrington, *Toward a Demo-*

cratic Left (New York: Macmillan Company, 1936), *p. 303:* 16–17

Khrushchev, Nikita, 52

King, Martin Luther, Jr., in Arthur M. Schlesinger, Jr., *A Thousand Days* (Boston: Houghton Mifflin Company, 1965), *p. 950:* 27

Kissinger, Henry A., *American Foreign Policy* (New York: W. W. Norton, 1969), *p. 29:* 34–35

Kopkind, Andrew, 66

Korea, 46, 177

Korean war, 40, 42–43, 52, 55

Ku Klux Klan, 62–63

Labor: blacks in unions, 150
  in party coalition, 150–151, 155

Labor party, British, 174

La Follette, Robert M., 141

Laissez-faire, 96

Laos, 36, 46

Lasch, Christopher, *The Agony of the American Left* (New York: Alfred A. Knopf, 1969), 145

Laski, Harold J., 98
  "The Obsolescence of Federalism," *The New Republic,* May 3, 1939, *pp. 367–369:* 130–131

Latin America, U.S. policy, 37–38

Leadership, 162–181
  intellectual, 164–167
  lack of confidence in, 162–163
  participatory, 167–171
  presidential, 169–179

Lenin, Nikolai, 73

Lerner, Max, "The Decade of Too Much," *Boston Herald Traveler,* Dec. 30, 1969, *p. 13:* 4

Lester, Julius, *Look Out Whitey! Black Power's Gon' Get Your Mama!* (New York: Evergreen, 1969), *p. 38:* 6

Liberalism: in American credo, 93–94
  economic issues, 16–17
  Ortega y Gasset on, 19

Liberal party, 142

Liberty: in American credo, 95–96
  equality in, 98–103
  in equality, 95–97

Lincoln on, 97
  negative, 96, 103–104
  positive, 97–98, 104
  as priority, 13
  Roosevelt's Four Freedoms, 39, 97–98
  values of, 103–105

Lilienthal, David, *The Harvest Years* (New York: Harper & Row, 1971), *p. 154:* 106–107

Lincoln, Abraham, 20–22, 144
  blacks, attitude toward, 20–22
  on Civil War: in Richard Hofstadter, *The American Political Tradition* (New York: Vintage Books, 1954), *p. 131:* 22
  on Civil War: in John G. Nicolay and John Hay, eds., *Complete Works of Abraham Lincoln* (Lincoln Memorial University, 1894), *vol. 10, p. 66:* 20
  on liberty: speech at Sanitary Fair, 1864, quoted by Roosevelt Oct. 23, 1940: Samuel I. Rosenman, ed., *The Public Papers and Addresses of Franklin D. Roosevelt* (New York: Macmillan Co., 1941), *p. 484:* 97
  on object of government, quoted in Robert J. Donovan, *Eisenhower: The Inside Story* (New York: Harper & Brothers, 1956), *p. 208:* 102
  on opportunity: speech of Mar. 6, 1860, in John G. Nicolay and John Hay, eds., *Complete Works of Abraham Lincoln,* op. cit., *vol. 5, p. 360–361:* 100
  on slavery: in Roy P. Basler, ed., *The Collected Works of Abraham Lincoln* (New Brunswick, N.J.: Rutgers University Press, 1953), *vol. 5, p. 388:* 21

Lindblom, Charles E., 91

Lindsay, John V., 138, 155
  becomes a Democrat, 142, 159
  on coalition of parties: *The New York Times,* Aug. 29, 1971, *p. 31:* 159

Little Rock, Ark., 26

Local government, 121, 130–135
  regional agencies proposed, 132–138
Long, Huey, 171
Los Angeles, politics, 142
Lowi, Theodore J., *The End of Liberalism* (New York: W. W. Norton, 1969), *pp. ix, xi*: 121; *p. 193*: 130
Lynching, legislation against, 24
Lynd, Robert S.: on cultural status: *Knowledge for What?* (Princeton: Princeton University Press, 1939), *p. 230*: 82
  on time outlook: *Knowledge for What?* op. cit., *pp. 1–2*: 12

MacLeish, Archibald, *The Saturday Review*, Aug. 29, 1970, *p. 16*: 15
Madison, James, 114–115, 143, 148
  Federalist 51, 115
Marcuse, Herbert, 62
  on civil liberties: in Robert Paul Wolff, Barrington Moore, Jr., and Herbert Marcuse, eds., *A Critique of Pure Tolerance* (Boston: Beacon Press, 1965), *p. 100*: 64–65
Marshall, Thurgood, 28
Maverick, Maury, 103
McCarthy, Eugene, 158
McCloskey, Robert G., *American Conservatism in the Age of Enterprise* (Cambridge: Harvard University Press, 1951), *p. 4*: 99
McGovern-Harris Commission, 157–158
McKinley, William, 144
Means and ends, *see* Ends and means
Mehl, Lucien, in Herman D. Stein, *Social Theory and Social Invention* (Cleveland: Press of Case–Western Reserve University, 1968), *p. 20*: 108
Middle class, 151
Military-industrial complex, 118
Miller, Perry, 93
Mills, C. Wright, 13, 118

The Sociological Imagination (New York: Oxford University Press, 1959), *p. 85*: 11
  White Collar (New York: Oxford University Press, 1951), 151
Monroe, James, 36
Morgenthau, Hans J.: on equality: *The Purpose of American Politics* (New York: Random House, 1964), Chap. 1: 96
  on foreign policy: *A New Foreign Policy for the United States* (New York: Frederick A. Praeger, 1969), *p. 242*: 176–177
  on intellectuals: "Truth and Power," *The New Republic*, Nov. 26, 1966, *pp. 8–14*: 164–165
  on political tradition: *The Purpose of American Politics*, op. cit., *p. 297*: 114
  on president: *The Purpose of American Politics*, op. cit., *p. 317*: 53–54
Morison, Elting E., Introduction, in Elting E. Morison, ed., *The Letters of Theodore Roosevelt* (Cambridge: Harvard University Press, 1952), *vol. 5, p. xvii*: 23
Morocco, 36
Morse, Wayne, 155
Moynihan, Daniel Patrick, privately circulated memorandum, 48
Muskie, Edmund, 142, 147
Mylai trial, ix
Myrdal, Gunnar: on Americans: *An American Dilemma* (New York: Harper & Brothers, 1944), *p. 1023*: 180–181
  on moral valuations: *An American Dilemma*, op. cit., *p. 1034*: 93, 106
  on principle of cumulation: *An American Dilemma*, op. cit., *p. 1067*: 84–85

Nader, Ralph, "Making Congress Work," *The New Republic*, Aug. 21 and 28, 1971, *pp. 19–21*: 126

National Advisory Commission on Civil Disorders, *Report* (New York: Bantam Books, 1968), 89

National Advisory Commission on Rural Poverty, *The People Left Behind*, 87

National Commission on Urban Problems, *Building the American City* (New York: Frederick A. Praeger, 1969), 88

National Labor Relations Board, 108

National Resources Planning Board, 122

Negroes, *see* Blacks

Neuhaus Richard J., in Peter L. Berger and Richard J. Neuhaus, *Movement and Revolution* (Garden City, N.Y.: Doubleday & Co., 1970), *pp. 163–232*: 66

New Deal, 101, 173

New Freedom, 100

New Frontier, 98

New Left, 51, 58, 59, 73

New York City: political parties, 142 suburbs, 131

Nixon, Richard M., ix, 6, 19, 30–32, 130, 142, 153
  China, visit to, 48
  and civil rights, 28–29
  economic strategy, 17–18
  federal agencies, reorganization, 123, 126–127
  "new American revolution," 59
  Supreme Court nominations, 29, 175
  Vietnam policy, 46–48, 55
  welfare reform, 79

No-monolith dogma, 51–53

Office of Management and Budget, 123

Oglesby, Carl, "Trapped in a System," in Matthew F. Stolz, ed., *Politics of the New Left* (Beverly Hills, Calif.: Glencoe Press, 1971), *p. 19*: 57

O'Hara Commission, 158

Ohlin, Lloyd E., *see* Cloward, Richard

Opportunity: equality of, 99–102 programs for, 101–103

Ortega y Gasset, José, *The Revolt of the Masses* (New York: W. W. Norton, 1932), *p. 83*: 19

Orwell, George, *1984*, 104

Paine, Thomas, 9
  Common Sense, in Philip S. Foner, ed., *The Complete Writings of Thomas Paine* (New York: The Citadel Press, 1945), *p. 17*: 5

Panama Canal zone, 38

Parrington, Vernon, 93

Parties, political, 139–161
  changes, possibility of, 145–149
  in cities, 142
  coalition proposed, 149–153, 172
  in Congress, 124–125, 146–147
  fitness to govern, 153–161
  fourth proposed, 141
  history of, 143–144
  independent voters, 140–141
  minor, 142, 145
  third, 141, 144–145, 152
  see also Democratic party; Republican party

Patriotism, anti-patriotic dogma, 51

Peirce, Charles S., 8

Pennock, J. Roland, *Liberal Democracy* (New York: Rinehart & Co., 1950), *p. 80*: 98

"Pentagon Papers," 44

Phillips, Kevin P., *The Emerging Republican Majority* (Garden City N.Y.: Doubleday & Co., 1969), 145

Plessy v. *Ferguson*, 166

Poland, 42, 52

Political parties, *see* Parties, political

Populists (People's party), 144, 145

Poverty: abolition of, 13, 78–79, 86, 121, 135–136
  inequality and, 82–83
  opportunity programs and, 102–103
  power and, 120
  rural, Advisory Commission reports, 87–88
  in transformation of government, 113–114
  War on, 17, 28, 79, 102

Power groups, 119–120

Pragmatism, 9–10, 19
  as American ideology, 93, 108
  in foreign policy, 34
Presidency, 8
  anti-presidential power dogma,
    53–54
  black problems and, 22–30
  civil rights and, 25–30
  Congress and, 53, 124–125, 172,
    175
  economic problems and, 30–32
  Electoral College and, 119
  executive branch, reform of, 126–
    129
  fiscal authority of, 123–124
  foreign policy and, 36–40, 122,
    169, 176–179
  leadership of, 169–179
  1972 campaign, 174–175
  planning and, 122–123
  strengthening of, 122–124
  weakness of, 32–33
  Wilson on, 176
Priorities, 13–14, 121
Progress, 16–33
Protests, 57–58
  on Vietnam war, 49, 58, 72–73
Pueblo incident, 40

Randolph, A. Philip, 24–25
Reform, 6
  change and, 81–83, 90–91
  of government, proposals, 121–129
Reich, Charles, The Greening of
    America (New York: Random
    House, 1970), p. 1: 59
Republican party, 8, 143, 146–149,
    154–155
  in Congress with southern Demo-
    crats, 160
  governors, 140
  history of, 143–144
  in New York City, 142
  Republicans in Democratic party,
    158–159
  weakness of, 155
Revolution, 56–73
  blacks in, 57, 66–71, 73
  character of revolutionaries, 57–59
  civil liberties and, 64–65, 67
  ends and means in, 60, 63, 65–68

  goals, statements of, 65–66, 69
  meaning of, 58–65
  rejection of American system, 56–
    58, 61
  and Vietnam war opposition, 72–
    73
  violence in, 60–64
Revolution, American, 57, 114
Riots, 18, 69
  causes of, 87, 89
  rural poverty and, 87
Roosevelt, Eleanor, 24, 25
Roosevelt, Franklin D., 27–28, 31,
    55, 122, 127, 146, 153, 173
  on anti-lynching bill: in Arthur
    M. Schlesinger, Jr., The Politics
    of Upheaval (Boston: Hough-
    ton Mifflin Co., 1960), pp. 437–
    438: 24
  blacks, attitude toward, 24–25
  Democratic party coalition, 144,
    145
  foreign policy, 38–40
  Four Freedoms, 39, 97–98
  letter to Hopkins, in James M.
    Burns, Roosevelt: The Soldier of
    Freedom (New York: Harcourt
    Brace Jovanovich, 1970), p.
    450: 168
  poverty programs, 78, 79
  The Public Papers and Addresses
    of Franklin D. Roosevelt, ed. by
    Samuel I. Rosenman (New York:
    Macmillan Co.), 1941 vol., p.
    484: 97; 1944–1945 vol., pp.
    40–41: 97–98; 1944–1945 vol.,
    pp. 570–586: 39–40
  Supreme Court and, 175
  United Nations, proposal for, 40
  in World War II, 38–39
Roosevelt, Theodore, 78, 100, 141
  blacks, attitude toward, 22–23
  on Booker T. Washington: in
    George M. Fredrickson, The
    Black Image in the White Mind
    (New York: Harper & Row,
    1971), p. 300: 23
  foreign policy, 36–38
Rubin, Jerry, Do It! (New York:
    Ballantine Books, 1970), p.
    148: 6

Rumania, 41
Russia: T. Roosevelt's policy on, 36–37
see also Soviet Union
Russo-Japanese War, 36

Scammon, Richard M., and Ben J. Wattenberg, *The Real Majority* (Coward-McCann, 1970), rev. ed. 1971, as discussed by Scammon, *The New York Times*, Aug. 27, 1971, *p. 56*: 160
Schlesinger, Arthur M., 93
School integration, busing, 29
Schultze, Charles L. *The Politics and Economics of Public Spending* (Washington: The Brookings Institution, 1968), *pp. 37–40*: 87; *p. 47*: 91
SDS (Students for Democratic Society), 69–70
Slavery: in Constitution and Declaration of Independence, 19–20
Lincoln on, 21
Smith, Alfred E., 153
SNCC, 163
Socialist party, 153
Soledad Brothers, 71
South Africa, 36
Southeast Asia, *see* Vietnam war
Soviet Union: China and, 51–52
communist regimes established, 50
Czechoslovakia, invasion of, 43, 52
dissent in, 52
in Korean war, 52
U.S. foreign relations, 41
in Vietnam war, 44, 52
Spencer, Herbert, 96
Square Deal, 100
Stevenson, Adlai, 147, 174
Students: opinions on American system, 3
as revolutionaries, 65–66, 70
as voters, 139
Students for Democratic Society (SDS), 69–70
Suburbs, 131, 141
Suez crisis, 40
Sundquist, James L., *Politics and Policy* (Washington: The Brookings Institution, 1968), *p. 54*: 123
Supreme Court, 107, 108
Brown v. *Board of Education*, 166–167
Nixon nominations, 29, 175
Plessy v. *Ferguson*, 166
Roosevelt and, 175
under Warren, 166–167

Taft, William Howard, 38
Tawney, Richard H., 87, 99
Equality (New York: Harcourt, Brace & Co., 1931), 82
Taxes: reduction, 123
sharing, 129–130
Thoreau, Henry David, 13
Tocqueville, Alexis de, 98
on American credo: *Democracy in America*, ed. by J. P. Mayer and Max Lerner (New York: Harper & Row, 1966), *pp. 144–148*: 93
on Constitution: op. cit., *p. 150*: 129
Tonkin, Gulf of, 40
Transformation of government, 113–138
Truman, Harry S., 31, 145
and civil rights, 25
poverty programs, 78, 79
Turkey, 37, 42

U-2 incident, 40
Udall, Stewart, *1976: Agenda for Tomorrow* (New York: Harcourt, Brace & World, 1968), *p. 81*: 6
Ulam, Adam B.: on dissent in Soviet Union: *The Rivals* (New York: Viking Press, 1971), *p. 433*: 52
on dogmas: *The Rivals*, op. cit., *p. 392*: 50
Unions: blacks in, 150
in political action, 150–151
United Nations, 36, 40–42

Values: American system of, 92–95
as guides to action, 105–110
hierarchies of, 106–108

Values (cont'd)
  of liberty and equality, 103–105
  moral, Myrdal on, 93, 106
Vietnam: coalition government proposed, 49
  partition of, 45
Vietnam, North, 51
  Soviet Union and China support, 44, 52
  U.S. policy on, 43
  in war, 46–48
Vietnam, South, U.S. policy on, 42–45
Vietnam war, 40, 43, 122, 177
  Nixon's policy, 46–48, 55
  political impact, 143
  protests against, 49, 58, 72–73
  Tet offensive, 44, 46
  U.S. policy, 42–49, 54–55
  Vietnamization, 46–48
  withdrawal of U.S. forces, 46–49
Villard, Oswald Garrison, 23
Violence: Berrigan on, 61–63
  in revolution, 60–64
Von Vorys, Karl, "The Concept of National Interest," in Vernon Van Dyke, ed., Some Approaches and Concepts Used in the Teaching of International Politics (Iowa City: State University of Iowa, 1957), pp. 49–54: 109
Voters: black, 141–142, 144–145, 150, 154–155
  independent, 140–141
  middle class, 151
  young, 139, 143, 150, 151, 154
  see also Parties, political

Wallace, George, 29, 141, 142, 153
War on Poverty, 17, 28, 79, 102
Warren, Earl, 25, 166–167
Warren, Sidney, The President as World Leader (Philadelphia: J. B. Lippincott Co., 1964), pp. 79, 85: 37–38
Washington, Booker T., T. Roosevelt on, 23
Washington, George, 36
Washington, march on: 1941, proposed, 24–25
  1963, 27–28
Wattenberg, Ben J., see Scammon, Richard M.
Watts riot, 118
Weathermen, 62–63, 69
Welfare Rights Movement, 71
Whigs, 144
White, Walter, 24, 25
Wilson, Woodrow, 25, 78, 100, 153
  blacks, attitude toward, 23–24
  foreign policy, 37–38
  on presidency: in Sidney Warren, The President as World Leader (Philadelphia: J. B. Lippincott Co., 1964), p. 79: 176
  World War I message, 37–38
Women's Liberation, 59, 71
World War I, Wilson in, 37–38
World War II, 55
  Roosevelt in, 38–39
  U.S. occupations after, 177–178

Youth: leadership rejected by, 163
  as revolutionaries, 57–58, 62–63, 70–71
  violence of, 62–63
  as voters, 139, 143, 150, 151, 154
Yugoslavia, 41

Zinn, Howard, "Marxism and the New Left," in Priscilla Long, ed., The New Left: A Collection of Essays (Boston: E. N. Sargent, 1969), p. 59: 72